TRULY
Walking
WITH GOD

GEORGE D. VITETTA
with Catherine M. Vitetta

ISBN: 978-1-951280-41-3

DEDICATION & ACKNOWLEDGEMENTS

As always, I would like to dedicate this book first and foremost to the one true living God, who originated the book's concept, developed it, and brought it to completion!

I would also like to give a special word of thanks to my pastors and brothers in Christ, Pastor Tom Patterson and Pastor Dan Hudson. Their friendship, guidance, counsel, and support have been a huge blessing from the Lord.

Finally, I would like to thank Manifest International for their prayer-filled guidance and assistance in organizing the gathered materials into a coherent, published book.

To God be all glory!

Contents

Preface, *by Catherine*   i

Introduction, *by George*   1

Section 1: Background Story

God's Hand Upon My Life: the Highlights   5
by George

Highlights Continued, *by Catherine*   21

**Section 2: Why the Crucifixion & Resurrection?
A 5-Part Series**

Part 1 of 5: The Stage is Set   29

Part 2 of 5: Do You Really Know Jesus?   41

Part 3 of 5: The Veil is Torn   56

Part 4 of 5: He Has Risen   66

Part 5 of 5: Reconnected Back to God   77

Section 3: Foundation for the Christian Life

Are You the Light?   91

Is Grace the Right to Sin?   101

The Desires of Our Heart   114

Who is My Brother & Sister?   128

Closing Thoughts &Prayer, *by Catherine*   135

Afterword: George's Last Day   137
by Catherine

PREFACE

by Catherine

A few short years ago, the Lord placed it on my husband's heart to write a book about his individual journey which resulted in a personal relationship with Christ Jesus. This book was to be about his life's journey and the change he experienced when he went from hearing and knowing things **about** God to having a personal relationship with the living God for himself. He knew that the Lord wanted him to write this down so that it could be of benefit to other people who also wanted and needed a real connection with God.

Then one day, George met with a fellow pastor at his favorite coffee house. It was their first time meeting each other and they knew nothing about one another, but in the midst of their conversation, the pastor's face became quizzical and said to George, "I have no clue what this is about, but the Lord wants me to ask you how the book is coming?" George chuckled and said "Well, let's just say, I better get going on it!" Thankfully, George started writing this book and assembled the significant teachings that he wanted to include.

As George looked back on his life and prayerfully considered what was to be included in this book, one of the many things that he realized was that God's hand was on him from the time he was born, even long before George really knew anything about God. Although George's early life was filled with pain and adversity, George could see in hindsight that the Lord's hand of provision was with him, even during those storms of life. He also recognized how the Lord could use his weaknesses and traumatic life experiences for good and for helping others as George fulfilled God's Kingdom purposes for and through his life.

As George considered how his walk towards and with the Lord evolved over the course of his life, he realized that not being well versed in gospel and biblical truths, whether due to incorrect or false teachings or his personal ignorance, was a huge stumbling block in finding and achieving a relationship with the one true living God. It was George's heart to ensure to the best of his ability that others would not struggle with these issues as he had, and that through reading this book your time of struggle could be minimized or avoided altogether!

George had all the pieces in place to complete

the writing of this book when the Lord took him home. George was 65 years old at the time of his passing. The story of his last day in this world is included at the end of this book. The Lord had told George that his time to go was coming soon, but for the rest of us it was sudden. He is greatly missed.

Following the initial phases of shock and grief that I experienced after George's physical death, the Lord placed it on my heart to finish the book that George had started. Completing this book has been a challenge for me, but it has also brought me immeasurable joy and a peace that surpasses all understanding, knowing that God's will for George's book is being fulfilled. I cannot put into words how much the Lord has blessed me through the process of completing what my beloved husband had started for the Lord.

I would like you to know that George and I spent many hours talking about what he believed was to be included in this book. George left behind his outline for the book, sermon notes, and tapings of his sermons that he intended to include. This book has been prayerfully and joyfully completed out of love for and obedience to the Lord and out of love for my husband and the message he proclaimed. All gratitude, honor and glory goes to our Lord Jesus!

George touched many, many lives for the Lord, including mine. It is my hope and prayer that reading this book blesses you as it has blessed me.

INTRODUCTION

by George

I [George] was inspired to write this book when I realized that my walk with God had finally come to a place where I was **truly** walking with Him. It was what I had always wanted but could not seem to find.

For roughly forty years I struggled with "religion" and all that it means. What I mean by this is that I wanted a real relationship with God, but I struggled with many false doctrines of legalism that can be so prevalent in today's church. These teachings ranged the gamut from telling me that I was going to Hell if I wore a short sleeve shirt or had a mustache all the way to it is "ok to sin" because I am human and God understands. The only thing that I was certain of during those years of searching for God was that I yearned to serve God with all my heart, mind, soul, and substance. But everything else seemed like a maze of confusion and a wilderness of wandering in search of the truth.

It pains my heart to see so many Christians falling away from the faith because they are lost in the wilderness of the same false doctrines that confused me and hindered my connection with God. The teachers of these false doctrines tickle the ears of their willing listeners by telling them just what they want to hear or to ensnare them with legalistic bondages. Usually, these false teachers are more concerned about numbers of people in the seats, money, and fame than they are about the souls and eternal destiny of the people they teach. In the end, after the false teaching proves to be a lie and does not produce the results the listeners were hoping for, many people become disheartened about Christianity and fall away from any sort of faith in the true God of the Bible. Others continue searching and learning but are never able to reach the fullness of God and a real relationship with Him. They have a form of godliness but deny the power God gives us by His Holy Spirit.

I want to make one thing clear. I am no different than anyone else who is struggling to serve God in a world that vexes your soul every second of every day. What I can honestly tell you is that in the midst of the storms of life, you **can** have a peace and joy that surpasses all understanding. You **can** have a relationship with the living God through His Holy Spirit!

You can **truly** walk with God!

SECTION 1:

BACKGROUND STORY

George recognized that God's hand had been upon his life long before he came to know and acknowledge Jesus as his Lord and Savior. He was thankful that God knew him even before he knew God.

GOD'S HAND UPON MY LIFE, THE HIGHLIGHTS

by George

I was born on October 8, 1956, in Albany, NY, at the beginning of the seventh month of gestation. Most children born at this early stage did not survive, as the medical technology of today simply did not exist back then. I was the exception, however, not the norm. I see in hindsight that God truly had his hand on me from the beginning. But my life as a child was not going to be easy. In fact, sometimes it was going to be excruciatingly painful. The fact that I am still alive and serving God is a miracle and a testament to His grace and love!

One of my earliest memories as a child was when I was in preschool. My family and I visited a camp site in upstate New York. We were gathered around a large firepit in which a fire had been burning most of the day. At the end of the day, some very hot embers and ash were all that was left in the pit. Apparently, I was standing near it when one of my uncles ran into me, accidentally knocking me into the fire pit. He quickly tried to pick me up out of the pit, but I slipped through his hands and was accidentally dropped back onto those burning embers a second time.

My parents rushed me to the hospital, but all I can remember to this day was watching the doctor cut the blackened skin off of my legs. I had first, second, and third degree burns from my waist down. At this time in the late 1950's, there were no specialized burn care units like there are today. There was only God. Today, I can proudly testify that I have no physical scars on my body because God healed my body completely! Only the memory of the burns remains.

A year or two after that incident, I became very ill and had significant difficulty breathing. I was rushed to the hospital where an emergency tracheotomy was performed. I remember waking up in an oxygen tent with crude wires attached to me. I don't remember everything that happened to me there, but the effects of going without oxygen were evident.

Afterwards, I had a problem maintaining my focus and my speech became impaired. My parents brought me home from the hospital and tried to take care of me but felt that they were unable to do so.

I went through several evaluations over the

following months. There was one exam that I distinctly remember to this day. I had to look at ink blots and describe what I thought they looked like. I had to do this several times. I became very annoyed with the examiner and just made up random answers. After my evaluations were completed, it was decided it would be best to place me in a facility that specializes in caring for special needs and troubled children.

At this facility, I only had a bunk for a bed and a foot locker where the few things I had could be stored. I recall eating meals in a dining hall and could only see my parents once a week for an hour. On special occasions, like Christmas, I was allowed to go home for the weekend.

I spent two long years there. One memory that remains was the tall fence that surrounded the property of the facility. I remember standing at the fence and looking out at the other children walking home from school. I wished I was them! I just stood there crying because it felt like I was being caged like an animal. I felt so abandoned.

Also at that facility, I endured things that a child shouldn't have to endure. The facility housed children up to the age of sixteen. Some of the older, emotionally troubled residents would treat the younger children with brutality. I remember being abused and forced to commit sexual acts. These particular memories haunted me for a long, long time. I became so depressed that all I did was eat. I ballooned up to 177 pounds by the time I was seven!

When I turned eight, I was finally allowed to go home and live with my family. Unfortunately, my excessive weight and speech impairment made me an easy target for teasing when I returned to the public school. The kids at school would laugh at me and torment me on a daily basis. I just wanted so much to be loved and accepted for who I was.

A couple of years later when I was roughly ten years old, I was struck by a car. I do remember being hit, as well as getting up and walking to the neighbor's porch and sitting down afterwards. My mother likes to tell the story that one of my friends knocked on the door and told her that someone had hit me. My mother, thinking that another boy had hit me, told my friend to tell me to hit him back! My friend replied "No, you don't understand, a car hit George and sent him flying like superman!" How I managed to stand up and walk to the porch was a miracle. Plus, I only had a bump on my head and a scratch on my shoulder. One eyewitness had told my mother that what was strange was that after I sat down on the porch, I fell over like someone had let go of me! Years later, I was telling a Christian friend about this incident, and they replied that it was probably an angel that helped me out of the street and onto the porch. Whether that is true or not, I don't know. But what I truly know now in hindsight is that God intervened and saved my life once again on that day!

A short while later while I was in 5th grade, my teacher put me up against the wall in front of the class. She was so irritated at me for not being able to pronounce my words properly, that she grabbed my jaw and proceeded to move it around saying, "This is how you talk!" It is a harsh memory, but truthfully, until I reached High School, I was not a good student. I was disruptive in class, and I just didn't care about doing any of my work assignments. Consequently, I was considered below average in my learning ability and was placed in what they called a slow tract for special needs children.

I was still very overweight at that time. In spite of this, I tried out for the Babe Ruth Baseball team. I made the team, but they couldn't find a uniform that would fit me because of my excessive weight. Still today, my sister's father-in-law, who was my Babe Ruth Baseball coach, always lovingly chuckles about how large I was! For most of my childhood, I was constantly ridiculed and put down because I was so different from my peers! I wanted so much to fit in but never seemed to be able to do so.

During the course of these years, I was an altar boy at the Catholic Church. I loved serving the Lord and felt a sense of belonging there while I was serving in the Church. It was there that I first learned about Jesus and what Jesus did for me on the cross. It was there that I started to develop a curiosity about the Lord and a sense of love for Him. However, this was also the place where man-made rules and regulations brought me into confusion about what God was really like and what He wanted from me. Furthermore, on one occasion, a priest taught that the Catholic Pope was infallible and never makes mistakes. But in the same time frame, the priest taught that someone who had been acknowledged as a saint by a prior Pope was now deemed not to be a saint by the current Pope. When I asked the Priest which infallible Pope was wrong (because they had reached different conclusions), the Priest rebuked me for being greatly disrespectful and dismissed me from being an altar boy. To me, this rejection by the Priest and from service in the Church was equal to being rejected by God. As a result, I shut my mind and heart off from God for quite some time.

But while I was in middle school, someone came into my life that would change me forever. Her name was Miss Perkins. She was a kind, elderly teacher. Today, I understand that the Lord put her in my life and it was God who put me on her heart in a special way. In me, she saw a child that was different but had the potential to really excel in school. When everyone else had given up on me, Miss Perkins took the time to guide and help me whenever she could. I went from being in a special education class for slow students to the honor role in just one year. In fact, when someone congratulated my mother on my academic accomplishment, she replied, "You must be mistaken!" They had to show her the local newspaper which published the names of those who made the honor roll each semester.

Life during my mid-teens was fairly uneventful. Not only had I lost all of my excess weight, but I had become very athletic and self-confident. I was still different from others in the way that I perceived and thought about things, but now I was finally socially accepted by others in my age group. The world had finally accepted me, and I was no longer an outcast! My newfound social life became my primary focus – and it was

11

fun! I was not thinking about God at all during this time because life seemed fine enough without Him.

Immediately after high school in 1974, I joined the United States Air Force. I excelled in my training to become an aircraft mechanic by the time I was twenty years old. While I was still stationed at my training facility in Wichita Falls, Texas, I married my high school sweetheart. It seemed that I was on top of the world and life was going to be great from here on out. After my training was completed, I was stationed at Webb Airforce Base in Big Springs, Texas. Again, I excelled at everything they gave me to do and became the youngest assistant dock chief on the Base. Within two years of service, I had attained the rank of Sargent and it appeared that I had a promising career in the military.

Life was good! Little did I know that things were about to change in my life in a way that I never could have anticipated.

A LIFE CHANGING MOMENT

One of my service friends, Glenn, was associated with a Holiness Church in town. He started witnessing to me about God and invited me to his church. I remember the first time I went to a service out of curiosity - I left thinking that these people were truly nuts! They were shouting, dancing, and speaking in an unknown language which made me feel very uncomfortable. But I couldn't deny the feeling of what I now know to be the corporate presence of the Holy Spirit! I had never experienced anything like it before. Yet, I knew I wanted more of it but was unsure how to obtain it.

I kept hearing them talk about having this personal relationship with Jesus Christ. They preached salvation through repentance, adult baptism, and the infilling of the Holy Spirit. They believed that if you received the Holy Spirit, you would speak in tongues. From my Catholic upbringing, I knew that Jesus had died on the cross for my sins. However, speaking in tongues, healing the sick, and running the aisles seemed a little unorthodox to me. I find it ironic that I was skeptical about healings after all the times that God had already healed me!

But even though I was skeptical, I so desperately wanted to find God and have that personal relationship with Him that Glenn and others were talking about. Several times during alter calls, I would go to the front of the church for prayer. People prayed for me to receive the Holy Spirit, but it felt like nothing ever happened. I became discouraged and disillusioned.

Looking back, I think I was looking for the Holy Spirit to fill me in a power-encounter through the laying on of hands of other church members. I was waiting for the Holy Spirit to be poured into me through ministry rather than simply and earnestly desiring it in my heart and seeking it directly from the Lord.

Then one day at the peak of my frustration, I was alone at home and went on my face before the Lord. I prayed and cried and told the Lord that I was not going to leave until I was filled with His Holy Spirit! After a few hours, I realized I was no longer praying in the English language but was praying in an unknown tongue! I had finally been filled with the Holy Spirit of the living God with the evidence of speaking in tongues!

> *Matthew 7:7-8 - 7 Ask, and it shall be given you; seek, and ye shall find; knock, and it shall be opened unto you: 8 For every one that asketh receiveth; and he that seeketh findeth; and to him that knocketh it shall be opened.*

In 1977, after spending three-and-a-half years in the military, I was discharged under honorable conditions because I was deemed medically unable to perform my duties anymore. This was because there had been an explosion and fire in the plane hangar, and the outermost layers of both of my corneas were burned, among other injuries. I was told this severe injury to my eyes should have left me completely blind. But when the doctors took the bandages off my eyes, my vision was perfect! Medically speaking in the natural way of things, there was literally no explanation for my vision to be fully restored. I know now that it was the hand of God that saved my vision!

At this time, I had a young daughter, and my wife was pregnant with our son. With my military career now over, my family and I moved back to upstate New York. I had also become an active member of the Church and was being groomed to be a preacher. This Church taught us that God came first, church duties came second, then family came third, or last. To clarify, I now believe that it should be God first, family second, and church duties third. However, I was diligently following what I was being taught and I became totally focused on prioritizing and fulfilling my duties for the Lord and the Church. So much so, that I neglected my family and failed to meet their spiritual and emotional needs because I was spending so much time attending to the spiritual and emotional needs of others. Because of this, my marriage disintegrated and dissolved, resulting in divorce. The Church offered us no pastoral care or marriage counseling. I again felt rejected and abandoned by the Church in my time of need. As a result, I again shut my heart off to God. The Church had again hurt me, and it left a very bad taste in my mouth. I wanted nothing to do with God or the Church ever again.

Over the next ten or so years, I immersed myself in my work. I initially worked as a machinist at the Watervliet Arsenal, then as a lead weapons designer for the United States government. I also busied myself in activities of the world such as competitive bowling and being a lead singer in a local rock-n-roll band.

But after about ten years of living in the world without God, I was starting to feel empty once again. My past started to overwhelm me as the memories of my childhood started coming back to haunt me. In hindsight, it is most likely that I had blocked out a lot of what happened to me in those early years as a coping mechanism. My emotional stability became quite shaky with these childhood memories flooding my mind.

During this time, my focus was not on God at all. Living for God was not on my agenda. I had forgotten about feeling God's presence in the

Holiness Church and praying in tongues. However, as time progressed that year, I kept feeling this uneasiness inside me that I could not shake. I decided to just ignore it, assuring myself that in time it would pass. In hindsight, I know now that the encounter I had with the presence of God in that Holiness Church had left me with this nagging, empty feeling inside that would never be satisfied with anything or anyone but God Himself. No matter how much I tried to fill it with the activities and pleasures of this world, I could not shake the memory of that experience with God's presence.

At this point in the writing of the Introduction to this book, George went home to be with the Lord.

Some of you might be wondering why George chose to share these significant and seemingly random negative experiences of his life with all of you. He wanted all of you to know that even during the harsh and challenging storms of life, although he did not yet know God, or even when he had turned his heart away from God and the Church, God was still with him and looking out for him! Looking back, George could see God's hand of provision in each of those tragic situations as well as how God utilized the pain he suffered for later good.

And to this I can confidently add that because George experienced ultimate victory in his life through Christ, he was able to lead others to the Lord who had also suffered in this life into their own victories in Christ. It was beauty for ashes, just as scripture states!

> *Romans 8:28 – 28 And we know that all things work together for good to them that love God, to them who are the called according to [his] purpose.*

George's life witness was a shining example of the truth of this scripture! Because of those experiences, George could truly love and have compassion for others because he knew firsthand what it felt like to be beaten, ridiculed, confined, sexually abused, and rejected by the world. Only the Lord could take those incidents which were meant for George's harm and utilize them for good. To God be the glory!

> *2 Corinthians 12:9 – [The Apostle Paul quoting Jesus] And he said unto me, My grace is sufficient for thee: for my strength is made perfect in weakness. Most gladly therefore will I rather glory in my*

*infirmities, that the power of Christ
may rest upon me.*

George was a shining example of the truth of this scripture also. Remember how George suffered oxygen loss to the brain as a child and was left with attention issues and speech related deficits? God showed him how to effectively channel his attention and energy to learn and master anything he desired to accomplish. George went on to become highly capable in a broad range of skills. Through reading manuals and watching videos, he became capable in all aspects of carpentry, building, plumbing, electrical work, tiling, landscaping, masonry, welding, and I'm not sure what else! Because of this, people were always seeking out George's counsel for their projects and this opened countless opportunities for him to share about the Lord with them!

As for the speech related issues, George had an amazing mind and memory, but his grammar and spelling remained atrocious! However, God used George by having him write teachings and sermons and by having him do lots and lots of talking and preaching! George always gave all the credit for his skills and accomplishments to the Lord. He knew where he had come from and what he had come through. He knew that it was only possible because God used his weaknesses to make him strong.

God is a redeemer and a restorer! What an awesome God we serve!

HIGHLIGHTS CONTINUED

by Catherine

By the time I met George, he was long divorced and his children were young adults in their twenties. His daughter was married and had a baby daughter of her own. George decided to attempt to fill the emptiness he felt by dating. After several unsuccessful dates and a few relatively brief relationships, George was introduced to me by a mutual friend.

At the time when we met, I had been divorced for a few years and had a 10-year-old son. I was in the process of questioning my Catholic faith, thinking there has to be more to God than this! I was just discovering non-denominational, Bible-based Christianity. I had tons of questions, and George was a handsome man with lots of biblical knowledge. I was hungry for God, and my never-ending plethora of questions reignited George's love and passion for the Lord.

I like to believe that ours was a match made in Heaven! We were happily married for 17 years. Over those years, we gradually went from being regular church attendees, to leading Bible studies, to George being ordained as a Pastor. Eventually, we even had a small but sincere and Spirit-filled home church. It was so exciting to watch and experience God's will for us unfold as we lived our lives together for Him!

George took the responsibility of being a Pastor very, very seriously. George studied the Word of God every single day. He read the entire Bible several times throughout his life, and always cross-referenced with a variety of commentaries, as well as looked up the Greek and Hebrew roots of the words in scripture to understand the true depth and fullness of God's meaning and message. He loved teaching biblical truths!

Even though he was very serious about serving God and disciplining himself, George was very down to earth, practical, real and relatable with everyone he met. Even in his manner of dress when preaching in our home church, he always wore a button down, long-sleeve, solid colored shirt, jeans, and sneakers. There was nothing formal, unapproachable, or stuffy about him. He truly had the heart of a humble servant of the Lord.

But in spite of casual dress, George spoke for God with power and strength, delivering the truth directly and plainly with love. I must warn you that George preached the "meat" of the

Word of God with very little fluff, all while establishing repeated eye contact with each person attending the service. He always poured his heart out and gave his very best!

George began almost every service by showing a brief video clip which would set the stage for that day's sermon. He produced the videos himself as a teaching tool to help people connect with the reality of the teaching he was presenting from the Word of God.[1] Following the brief video clip, George always opened the service in prayer.

As George neared what was to be the end of his life here on earth, he had fully dedicated his life to serving the Lord and had finally achieved that personal relationship with Jesus Christ that he had always craved! This was roughly 40 years after his first experience of God's presence in that "crazy" Holiness Church! All the praise, honor, glory, and gratitude to the Lord for directing our steps and never giving up on us!

As he looked back on his life, he could see how negative life experiences, false teachings, his own ignorance of the truth as well as personal misunderstandings hindered his walk towards

---

[1] To view some of our videos and sermons, please visit: Remnant Church CJ on YouTube *(the R is in a pink circle)*

and with the Lord at times. Although he was so grateful for his salvation and relationship with the Lord in his latter years, it saddened him to know that it took roughly 40 years of his life to finally get it right.

It was his goal to do his best to ensure that it did not take others as long as it did him to truly find and have an intimate walk with the Lord. It was his desire to share his life and his journey towards a personal relationship with Christ Jesus to give each of you struggling out there the hope that only rests in Jesus. George wanted everyone to know that it truly does not matter what you have done or suffered in this life because there is redemption through Christ. When you come to the Lord and are filled with His Holy Spirit, the Lord will waste nothing that you have suffered and will use it ultimately for good, as only He can do. You can become a new creature in Christ! God is true to His word, and He will never leave nor forsake you.

I believe that this was also the primary reason that George chose to include the sermons that are contained in this book. He wanted to give others some parameters to follow when assessing their own walk with Christ and personal salvation.

Another reason that George assembled these particular sermons was because he was saddened by the innumerable number of self-professed Christians out there in the world who think that they are born-again and saved, when they are not. They have been deceived. Some are unknowingly following false teachings. Others intentionally seek out teachers who will tell them what it is they want to hear. Others are ignorant of what the Bible says because of their own lack of study or because they are new to the faith. Whatever the reason for the deception, it truly grieved George's heart to watch people wandering in a wilderness of deceptions and disappointments while longing for a real relationship with God.

It was George's prayer, as it is also mine, that through this book, you will find answers and guidance so that you can have your own relationship with the living God and that your time in the wilderness will be brief, if at all.

GEORGE'S PRAYER BEFORE EACH SESSION

"Dear Heavenly Father, as always, we come before you and ask you to open our hearts so we can receive your Word. Touch our ears so we may hear your Word, and touch our eyes so we may see your Word. Father, I ask you to help me to deliver your Word, as I cannot do it by myself. Heavenly Father, please anoint me from the top of my head to the soles of my feet that Your Word might go forth, not mine. Amen!"

WHY THE CRUCIFIXION & RESURRECTION?

This section of the book is comprised of a 5-part sermon series that George gave every year at the time surrounding Resurrection Sunday, known commonly as "Easter." It was truly my most favorite sermon series of his as it so clearly explained everything about the what, where, when, why, and how of the Bible story of the Gospel of Christ in a way that is easily understandable for most people.

George wanted everyone to have clear understanding of the Gospel so that they could truly appreciate what it is the Lord did for each and every one of us as His beloved creation. It was the desire of George's heart to draw others to Christ Jesus for their eternal salvation. In order to do this, we agreed that it was of the utmost importance that everyone have a clear understanding of who Jesus is, what He did for us, and why He had to do it as He did.

It is with great joy that I present George's sermon series to you now:

THE STAGE IS SET

PRE-SERMON VIDEO:

This video is a series of alternating images and black screen text. It starts with a black screen showing the words:

> IN THE BEGINNING,
> GOD CREATED THE HEAVENS AND THE EARTH.

Then, after a flash of bright light, the earth appears in the heavens. Another black screen with the words:

> INTO MAN AND WOMAN MADE IN HIS IMAGE,
> HE BREATHED LIFE.

Next, a close-up of an opened eye. Then, another black screen with the words:

> EAT FREELY OF ALL THE FRUIT THAT I HAVE GIVEN,
> BUT NOT OF THIS ONE TREE OR YOU WILL DIE.

Next, appears a beautiful garden with rays of warm sunshine shining through. The next black screen displays the words:

> THE SERPENT CAME AND SAID,
> "DID GOD SAY?"

Then the screen goes to black and these words appear:

"YOU WILL NOT DIE. YOU WILL BE LIKE GOD."

Following this, a close up of a hand picking an apple off of a tree branch. The black screen that follows reads:

THEY ATE. SIN SEPARATED US FROM GOD.
BUT GOD DID NOT LEAVE US HOPELESS.
- GENESIS 3:15.

Finally, a brief image of the crucified Christ before the screen fades to final black and the video ends.

————————————————

THE SERMON:

In order to understand why there even needed to be the crucifixion and the resurrection, we need to go back to the book of Genesis to see what happened there. Truly, this is where it all started!

> *Genesis 2:15-17 - 15 And the LORD God took the man, and put him into the garden of Eden to dress it and to keep it. 16 And the LORD God commanded the man, saying, Of every tree of the garden*

thou mayest freely eat: 17 But of
the tree of the knowledge of good
and evil, thou shalt not eat of it: for
in the day that thou eatest thereof
thou shalt surely die.

Since God is omniscient, He knew that man would disobey Him and sin. The above scripture states, "for **in** the day that you eat of it you shall surely die," NOT "if you maybe, someday eat." Therefore, many people question how Adam and Eve died that day because God said that "in the day" they disobeyed His command, they would surely die, not die sometime in the future. We need to dig deeper to see the fullness of what God meant when He said, "You shall surely die."

Genesis 3:1 - 1 Now the serpent was
more subtil than any beast of the field
which the LORD God had made.

I want to stop here to discuss what is meant by the word serpent. In Hebrew, the word used in Genesis 3 for the serpent comes from a root word which refers to the hiss of a serpent or that of a whisperer, enchanter, or deceiver. As such, we can interpret the word serpent as "one who deceives through enchantment." This means that the serpent in the Garden with Adam and Eve represents Satan, God's adversary.

31

Scripture says that the serpent was more subtle than any beast of the field, meaning more cunning than anything made upon the earth.

> *Genesis 3:2-3 - And he said unto the woman, Yea, hath God said, Ye shall not eat of every tree of the garden? 2 And the woman said unto the serpent, We may eat of the fruit of the trees of the garden: 3 But of the fruit of the tree which [is] in the midst of the garden, God hath said, Ye shall not eat of it, neither shall ye touch it, lest ye die.*

Eve knew that God not only said not to eat of the fruit of that tree, but don't even go near it, lest you die. I have a saying, "Why meet evil half way when it's capable of making the entire trip on its own?" The Amplified Bible says in Proverbs 27:12, "A prudent man sees evil and he hides himself to avoid it. But the naive continue on and are punished." This means that the naive are easily misled and suffer the consequences for it. The Bible is clear that we are not to commune with evil or give any opportunity to the devil. This is something the church and individual Christians need to take to heart in today's times!

> *Genesis 3:4-5 - 4 And the serpent said unto the woman, Ye shall not surely die: 5 For God doth know that in the day ye eat thereof, then your eyes shall be opened, and ye shall be as gods, knowing good and evil.*

In this segment of scripture, the serpent implies that either Eve has misunderstood God or that God lied to Eve! He planted seeds of doubt in Eve's mind. He then appealed to her pride and told Eve that she would be like God if she ate of the fruit of that tree.

Interestingly, today's world tells us that we are our own gods, and we can decide what is good and what is evil for ourselves. We are told that we each have our "own, individual truths" that cannot be disputed. Clearly, that age old serpent, the devil, still casts out lies and runs around seeking whom he can kill and destroy! He uses the same old tactics again and again.

> *Genesis 3:6-7 - 6 And when the woman saw that the tree [was] good for food, and that it [was] pleasant to the eyes, and a tree to be desired to make [one] wise, she took of the fruit thereof, and did eat, and gave also unto her*

husband with her; and he did eat. 7 And the eyes of them both were opened, and they knew that they [were] naked; and they sewed fig leaves together, and made themselves aprons.

The serpent deceived Adam and Eve through the lust of the flesh (good for food), the lust of the eyes (pleasant to look at), and the pride of life (desire to make oneself wise.) At the moment when they ate from the forbidden tree, Adam and Eve realized the consequences of their disobedience to God. I truly believe that in that instant they disobeyed God and their eyes were opened, both of them experienced an indescribable crushing void as they died spiritually and felt the consequence of being separated from God!

Genesis 3:8-9 - 8 And they heard the voice of the LORD God walking in the garden in the cool of the day: and Adam and his wife hid themselves from the presence of the LORD God amongst the trees of the garden. 9 And the LORD God called unto Adam, and said unto him, Where [art] thou?

In this verse, when God asked Adam, "Where are you?", God was not saying he didn't know where Adam was located physically, but that Adam and Eve were no longer one with Him. They had lost their connection to God! The moment they ate of the fruit, they had died **spiritually**, just as God had promised they would surely die in that day.

> *Genesis 3:10-14 - 10 And he [Adam] said, I heard thy voice in the garden, and I was afraid, because I [was] naked; and I hid myself. 11 And he said, Who told thee that thou [wast] naked? Hast thou eaten of the tree, whereof I commanded thee that thou shouldest not eat?*

Of course, God knew what Adam and Eve had done but He wanted them to confess their sin and disobedience before Him.

> *Genesis 3:12 - 12 And the man said, The woman whom thou gavest [to be] with me, she gave me of the tree, and I did eat.*

Imagine Adam saying to God, "It's your fault this happened, God, because you gave me this woman!" Can you imagine the absurdity of this?

35

> *Genesis 3:13 - 13 And the LORD God said unto the woman, What [is] this [that] thou hast done? And the woman said, The serpent beguiled me, and I did eat.*

Eve probably thought it didn't go so well when Adam tried to blame God. So, Eve decided to blame the serpent.

> *Genesis 3:14 - 14 And the LORD God said unto the serpent, Because thou hast done this, thou [art] cursed above all cattle, and above every beast of the field; upon thy belly shalt thou go, and dust shalt thou eat all the days of thy life:*

This does not mean we are talking only about an actual snake that slithers on its belly. It is also metaphorically telling Satan that he has just lost all the status he once held!

THE FOUNDATION FOR THE RESTORATION OF MANKIND

This is the beginning of how God promised to correct what went wrong with mankind in the Garden with Adam and Eve.

> *Genesis 3:15 - 15 And I will put enmity between thee and the*

> *woman, and between thy seed*
> *and her seed; it shall bruise thy*
> *head, and thou shalt bruise his heel.*

This scripture is saying that Satan and the woman will be enemies, and that this war will last for generations to come via their offspring or "seed." The woman's offspring is humanity. Satan's offspring includes fallen angels, demons, and humans who choose to follow him against God through sin. The ultimate offspring of the woman is Jesus who has the final victory over Satan. Satan will only "bruise his heel," doing some damage to Jesus, but Satan can never, nor will he ever, have the final victory! Victory belongs to Jesus!

> *Genesis 3:21 - 21 Unto Adam also*
> *and to his wife did the LORD God*
> *make coats of skins, and clothed*
> *them.*

This scripture speaks of the first sacrifice of animals and shedding of blood to cover their nakedness - or in other words, to cover their sin. However, this could not take away their sins, it could only cover their sins. Since that first animal sacrifice, the Bible reveals the need for a blood sacrifice to cover over and ultimately take away the sins of mankind so that fellowship with God can be restored.

Genesis 3:22-24 - 22 And the LORD God said, Behold, the man is become as one of us, to know good and evil: and now, lest he put forth his hand, and take also of the tree of life, and eat, and live for ever: 23 Therefore the LORD God sent him forth from the garden of Eden, to till the ground from whence he was taken. 24 So he drove out the man; and he placed at the east of the garden of Eden Cherubims, and a flaming sword which turned every way, to keep the way of the tree of life.

Since man no longer had access to the tree of life, the process of physical death was set in motion. Genesis 3:19 clearly states the outcome of human life on earth: "For dust you are, and to dust you will return." Man was already spiritually dead.

SUMMARY OF WHAT HAPPENED IN THE GARDEN:

1. Sin entered the world.

2. Man spiritually died the day of the first sin.

3. Due to sin, man was separated from God and could no longer be in his presence.

4. The first sacrifice of animals was done to cover their nakedness, or sin. This was the first evidence that God would **require** a blood sacrifice to atone for the sins of mankind.

5. Man was cast out of the Garden and away from the tree of life. This began the process of physical death for man where he would eventually return to the dust of the ground because he no longer had access to the Tree of Life in the Garden.

6. God already had a plan to save man from his sins in order to be reconnected back to him. Thank God for that!

In the following chapters, we will see man's redemption through the cross, the resurrection of Jesus, and the infilling of the Holy Spirit.

FINAL SLIDE IMAGE:

Picture the limp body of Jesus Christ on the cross with the scripture verse of John 3:16 written beside it.

> *John 3:16 – 16 For God so loved the world, that he gave his only*

> *begotten Son, that whosoever*
> *believeth in him should not perish,*
> *but have everlasting life.*

You don't have to wait until this 5-part sermon series is completed to give your life to believe in God's redemption and put your faith in Jesus. Because of the cross, resurrection, and infilling of the Holy Spirit, you can be spiritually reconnected back to God right now! First, you need to repent, which means to turn your back on sin and start living for Christ. It will cost you everything to follow Jesus, but Jesus gave everything to allow each one of us the opportunity to be reconciled back to Him.

NOTES FROM CATHERINE:

Growing up in the Catholic Church, I knew that Jesus had died for my sins. However, it never made sense to me *why* Jesus had to die on the cross for the forgiveness of my sins. Understanding the fullness of *why* caused me to fall more in love with Jesus and be more committed to Him as my Lord and Savior. I hope that the way in which George presents the *why* in this 5-part series bears the same fruit for you in your life. Amen!

DO YOU REALLY KNOW JESUS?

PRE-SERMON VIDEO:

Picture a huge stone wall with an arched entry into the city of Jerusalem during the times of Jesus. Then, a voice speaks the following:

*"The next day the great crowd gathered because they heard that Jesus was on His way to Jerusalem. They took palm branches and went out to meet Him. They shouted, 'Hosanna, blessed is He who comes in the name of the Lord! Blessed is the King of Israel!' They praised Him and celebrated His miracles, and with great expectation told everyone about Him. But, they did not **know** Him. They were waiting for someone who would rule with strength and fight. But He came as a humble servant. They wanted Him to finally bring their people glory, but He came so their lives could bring God glory! They wanted a general who would crush their enemies, but He came to teach them to love their enemies. They thought He would offer deliverance from*

their oppressors, but He came offering deliverance from sin. This crowd would soon realize that Jesus was not what they wanted, and they turned on Him. They did not realize that Jesus was what they needed. So as they yelled, 'Crucify Him!' Jesus was asked, 'Are You a King?' And He replied, 'I am not that kind of King.' His kingdom is not what you see here on earth, established by chaos and war."

Then the background music slowly reaches a crescendo and the following is heard:

His Kingdom is in our hearts, His Kingdom is truth, His Kingdom is goodness and righteousness. He is a humble King. He is a King of healing, forgiveness, and love. Today, we lift our voices and cry, "Hosanna, save us from our sin and dwell in our hearts! Hosanna, we worship you, Jesus Christ our King!!"

———————————————

THE SERMON:

The big question is, "Do you really know Jesus?" Do you? Did they know who Jesus was? To answer this question, we are going to focus on Jesus' triumphal entry into Jerusalem just days before His crucifixion. In our times, the day on which these events took place is known as "Palm Sunday."

It is interesting to note that within several days, the crowd went from shouting, "Hosanna" to "Crucify Him!" Why did this happen and who did they think He was? Most sermons on this day are taken from Matthew 21. However, to understand what really happened, we must take into consideration all of the accounts given by the apostles. There is an account of this story given in Matthew, Mark, Luke, and John. But in this segment, we are going to look more closely at John's and Matthew's accounts.

> *John 12:1-3 – 1 Then Jesus six days before the passover came to Bethany, where Lazarus was which had been dead, whom he raised from the dead. 2 There they made him a supper; and Martha served: but Lazarus was one of them that sat at the table with him. 3 Then took Mary a pound of ointment of spikenard, very costly, and anointed the feet of Jesus, and wiped his feet with her hair: and the house was filled with the odour of the ointment.*

Some background information about this scripture for us to consider: First, Lazarus had been raised from the dead by Jesus, but would return to the grave at a future time. Lazarus was not transformed like Jesus was in the resurrection when He conquered the grave only to never return to it. Second, Lazarus was a wealthy man, as evidenced by the fact that he was buried in a sepulcher. A sepulcher was a grave hewn out of stone which was very costly in that day. Also, Lazarus' sister Mary is the woman who anointed Jesus' feet with a pound of spikenard which was equal to about a year's wage for the average person at that time.

> *John 12:4-6 – 4 Then saith one of his disciples, Judas Iscariot, Simon's [son], which should betray him, 5 Why was not this ointment sold for three hundred pence, and given to the poor? 6 This he said, not that he cared for the poor; but because he was a thief, and had the bag, and bare what was put therein.*

Judas Iscariot was being deceptive by pretending to care about the poor when in actuality, he just wanted to line his own pockets. Judas was stealing from God! He was following

Jesus with the other disciples, but the Lord's teachings had not penetrated his heart. We could say that he was pretending to be a sheep, but he was truly a wolf in sheep's clothing. Judas, though following along with the disciples of Jesus, was actually working for Satan. This goes back to Genesis where it speaks of the war between the woman's seed and the serpent's seed that we discussed in the previous segment of this 5-part series.

> *John 12:7-8 – 7 Then said Jesus, Let her alone: against the day of my burying hath she kept this. 8 For the poor always ye have with you; but me ye have not always.*

Can you imagine the confusion that Jesus' statement might have caused the Apostles and the people that were with them? On the one hand, Jesus is speaking of his death and burial, and on the other hand they believe that He is the Messiah whom they know from scripture and must have eternal life! They must have wondered where He was going so that they would not always have Him with them.

> *John 12:9-13 – 9 Much people of the Jews therefore knew that he was there: and they came not for Jesus' sake only, but that they*

might see Lazarus also, whom he had raised from the dead. 10 But the chief priests consulted that they might put Lazarus also to death; 11 Because that by reason of him many of the Jews went away, and believed on Jesus. 12 On the next day much people that were come to the feast, when they heard that Jesus was coming to Jerusalem, 13 Took branches of palm trees, and went forth to meet him, and cried, Hosanna: Blessed [is] the King of Israel that cometh in the name of the Lord.

What is really interesting in this portion of scripture is that many of the Jews believed that Jesus was the rightful King of Israel, an earthly kingdom, who was sent to deliver them from the Roman oppression and occupation of that time. They expected Jesus to be a mighty warrior who would lead them to defeat the Romans by force and establish His earthly kingdom. They were right that this would be the fulfillment of God's Kingdom coming to the earth, but they were blind to who Jesus truly was and the purpose of His first coming.

> *John 12:14-15 – 14 And Jesus,*
> *when he had found a young ass,*
> *sat thereon; as it is written, 15 Fear*
> *not, daughter of Sion: behold, thy*
> *King cometh, sitting on an ass's*
> *colt. (Quoting Zechariah 9:9.)*

Zechariah prophesied roughly 700 years before Jesus' time that the Messiah would ride an unbroken colt. An unbroken colt represented purity because it had not been defiled by man riding on it. A king approaching a city riding on a donkey represented that he was coming in peace. A king approaching a city on a dark horse represented that he has come to conquer (war). A king coming on a white horse represented that he has already conquered, such as when Jesus returns as stated in the Book of Revelation. All of this is to say that the people of that time would have understood the meaning behind the mode of transportation Jesus chose for His entry into Jerusalem.

But did they really know who Jesus was? More importantly, do **we** truly know who Jesus is?

> *John 12:37-38 – 37 But though he*
> *had done so many miracles*
> *before them, yet they believed*
> *not on him: 38 That the saying of*
> *Esaias the prophet might be*

> *fulfilled, which he spake, Lord, who hath believed our report? And to whom hath the arm of the Lord been revealed?*

We need to get on our knees and thank the Lord that our eyes have been opened!

> *John 12:39-43 – 39 Therefore they could not believe, because that Esaias said again, 40 He hath blinded their eyes, and hardened their heart; that they should not see with [their] eyes, nor understand with [their] heart, and be converted, and I should heal them. 41 These things said Esaias, when he saw his glory, and spake of him. 42 Nevertheless among the chief rulers also many believed on him; but because of the Pharisees they did not confess [him], lest they should be put out of the synagogue: 43 for they loved the praise of men more than the praise of God.*

How many in today's world refuse to follow Jesus because they love the things of this world more than they love God? Today and in the final days to come, many professing to be

Christians will fail by denying Jesus in order to save their earthly lives and maintain their earthly comforts. Why? Because they do not truly know Him or who He is. If they did, they would repent. Their focus is on the things of this world. What they fail to realize is that the purpose of this life is about our eternal redemption back to God for the Kingdom to come!

> *Luke 19:41-44 – 41 And when he was come near, he beheld the city, and wept over it, 42 Saying, If thou hadst known, even thou, at least in this thy day, the things [which belong] unto thy peace! But now they are hid from thine eyes. 43 For the days shall come upon thee, that thine enemies shall cast a trench about thee, and compass thee round, and keep thee in on every side, 44 And shall lay thee even with the ground, and thy children within thee; and they shall not leave in thee one stone upon another; because thou knewest not the time of thy visitation.*

The word "to know" in this context means to commune with Him in an intimate way. There are many today who profess to believe in Jesus but don't actually know Him intimately or know how to commune with Him. They can quote the Bible and display that they might know *of* Him, but they do not have a relationship *with* Him! Let that not be us!

> *Matthew 7:21-23 – 21 Not every one that saith unto me, Lord, Lord, shall enter into the kingdom of heaven; but he that doeth the will of my Father which is in heaven. 22 Many will say to me in that day, Lord, Lord, have we not prophesied in thy name? and in thy name have cast out devils? And in thy name done many wonderful works? 23 And then will I profess unto them, I never knew you: depart from me, ye that work iniquity.*

This scripture stresses the importance of our obedience to God and His Holy Word. His Word says, "If you love Me, you will obey Me." (See John 14:15.) This scripture tells us that those who are disobedient, or practice sin, will not enter the Kingdom of Heaven! How many self-professed Christians out there today deny the power of God by saying, "It's too hard, I can't change, I will continue in sin because God understands!" That's what I hear out there in the world today!

Jesus came the first time to set us free from the wages of sin which began at the fall of Adam and Eve in the Garden. Although the day will come when He conquers all kingdoms of this world, His purpose for His first coming was to conquer sin, not the Romans. Without His coming, the whole world was doomed and there would be no hope of anyone being reconnected back to God.

Again I ask, do you truly know Jesus?

As we approach part three of this sermon series, which is the crucifixion, we must ask ourselves: What happened that caused the people of Jerusalem to welcome Jesus and hail Him as King one day, and then a few days later shout out in agreement to crucify Him?

When Jesus entered Jerusalem on the donkey with the people crying, "Hosanna, Hosanna in the Highest," one of the first things He did was go into the temple and cast out the money changers saying, "It is written, 'My house shall be called a house of prayer; but ye have made it a den of thieves.'" (See Matthew 21:13.) When He called the Jewish Temple, the House of God, "My House," He was actually proclaiming Himself to be God.

Shortly after all of this, the chief priests of the temple asked Jesus, "By whose authority do you say and do these things?" It was customary in that day to identify who your teacher or mentor was in order to validate your own credibility. Jesus replied that He would answer their question only if they could answer this one question from Him. He asked them, "The baptism of John, was it of Heaven or of men?" The chief priests could not and would not answer that question because if they said it was of Heaven, then they would have been asked why they did not believe or give credibility to John. But, if they said it was of man, the chief priests feared the reaction of the people as the people held John in high regard as a prophet.

The Pharisees and Sadducees were more interested in keeping their prestige, power, control, and comfortable lifestyles than investigating if Jesus truly was the Messiah. Their lives and livelihood were very much threatened. Therefore, they used the words of Jesus against Him to claim that He was guilty of blasphemy by calling Himself the Son of God.

The main question that is being asked of us is, "Do you really know Jesus?"

The Sadducees and the Pharisees did not care at all who Jesus truly was. All they cared about was themselves and what Jesus' presence in society meant to them and their carnal lives here on earth. Since the possibility existed that Jesus could be the Messiah, they reasoned that this could have a very negative impact on their worldly status and power. Therefore, they chose to get rid of Him once and for all.

How many of us do that today? I personally know people who avoid the Lord at all costs because it is more important to them to be able to do whatever they want, whenever they want in their carnal lives here on earth. They intentionally turn their back on Him and pretend He does not exist. In other words, God is "dead" to them. That is a very sad class of people!

FINAL SLIDE IMAGE:

Picture a slide with the crucified Christ on it with the words written, "Hosanna, save us!"

You can attend church every week for 40 years and still not know Jesus personally. Just like the Jews at the time of that first Palm Sunday, any one of us can claim to be a believer, but still not know Him or who He truly is, just like the Sadducees and Pharisees. I can sit in a garage for 40 years and say "beep-beep" but that does not mean that I am a car.

If you don't have a personal relationship with Jesus, Jesus made this promise: "If you love Me more than anything and obey me, I will send the comforter!" You will never feel lonely or empty again. He promises in His Holy Word that He will never leave us nor forsake us. And if you love Jesus in this way, His Holy Spirit will dwell inside of you. When we are infilled with the Holy Spirit, we can have a peace that surpasses all understanding in the midst of any storm we experience in our lifetime! Amen?

NOTES FROM CATHERINE:

The point George really wanted to make was that there is a huge difference between knowing the Lord intimately through a personal relationship with Him verses just knowing *of* Him. Even the devil knows of God and His Word, yet his eternity in Hell is already set. If you do not have a personal relationship with Christ through the infilling of His Holy Spirit, then you only know *of* Him and do not actually know Him!

We must be born again, which means that we are filled with God's Holy Spirit, in order to be saved and have the promise of eternal life with the Lord. God's Holy Word tells us that He must be the center of our lives, meaning that we put the will of God before our own will. If we truly put the Lord's will before our own will, then we will live a life of sacrificial obedience to the entire Word of God, plus to any individual directives He might give us once we have that personal relationship with Him.

It pained George to know people who spent hours studying the Word of God in the Bible to the point that they could accurately quote scriptures but continued to live a self-centered life in sin and disobedience for whatever the reason. These people have only head knowledge of God and His Word but do not know God in their hearts. Those who believe that God tolerates sin because we are not perfect and we can't help ourselves are deceived about God and His love. His love is not an excuse for sin but the means of overcoming it through faith in what Jesus has done for us. It weighed heavily on George's heart that these people believe themselves to be saved but will stand before the Lord and most likely hear, "Depart from me, I never knew you" because they never lived their lives by the transforming power of the Holy Spirit.

Do you have a personal relationship with the living God?

THE VEIL IS TORN

PRE-SERMON VIDEO:

The video starts with an excerpt from the film *The Passion of Christ*. Picture a close-up of the face of Mary, the mother of Jesus, looking up at the cross in deep anguish. Then, the view enlarges to include the bloodied and crucified Jesus on the cross at the moment of His physical death, when He looked upwards and uttered the words, "Father, into Your hands I commend My Spirit," and Jesus' head drops to His chest.

Then, what appears to be a teardrop from Heaven falls to the ground and a huge earthquake starts. The wind blows mightily and the people scatter in shock and fear.

The scene changes and we see the Temple of God shaking from the earthquake and the following words appear on the screen in capital letters:

THE VEIL OF THE TEMPLE
WAS RENT IN TWO!

Then, the scene shifts back to the cross at the

moment when the Roman soldier pierced our Lord and Savior's side with the spear.

Shifting back to the partially destroyed Temple, we see the Sadducees and Pharisees running around in shock and disbelief.

Finally, with the cross in view, we see the Roman soldier dropping to his knees and looking up at the crucified Christ. (We know from the scripture that in that moment, He declared, "Surely, this was the Son of God.")

THE SERMON:

The temple veil was torn in two! Today, we will look at what the veil represented and why the crucifixion of Christ was necessary.

> *Matthew 27:50-53 – 50 Jesus, when he had cried again with a loud voice, yielded up the ghost. 51 And, behold, the veil of the temple was rent in twain from the top to the bottom; and the earth did quake, and the rocks rent; 52 And the graves were opened; and many bodies of the saints which slept arose, 53 And came out of*

the graves after his resurrection, and went into the holy city, and appeared unto many.

In the Temple of God, a veil without seams was placed in the entry to the innermost room of the Temple. The innermost room was called the "Holy of Holies," and this was where God's presence resided in the Temple. So, what does the veil represent? The veil was a physical representation of man's separation from God due to sin. Light cannot coexist with darkness!

Under the Law of Moses, the High Priest was the only person allowed to enter behind the veil into the Holy of Holies to present a blood sacrifice to God for the atonement of the sins of man. Moreover, he could only do this once per year on Yom Kippur, the Day of Atonement, and only after he had gone through a specific purification process. If he did not perfectly follow God's instructions for purification, he would die once he entered the Holy of Holies. Everyone except for the High Priest and only on Yom Kippur, had to remain in the outer court of the Temple.

In light of this history, I am astounded today when people say they don't have to follow God's instructions or commandments! It certainly did not go well for the High Priest if he failed to fully comply with God's instructions! And since God is no respecter of persons, meaning he does not play favorites, why would we expect any less for our disobedience?

Again, the veil in the Temple was a physical representation of the fact that sin separated man from communion with God. When the veil in the Temple was torn as Jesus Christ died on the cross, it was the fulfilment of Genesis 3:15, which we talked about earlier in this 5-part series, and which is the foundation of our restoration back to God. Sin would no longer have dominion over us! By His blood we could be forgiven and, ultimately, reconnected back to God.

WHY THE CRUCIFIXION?

The blood of Christ, which was required for the ultimate forgiveness of the sin of man, was the sealing of the promise made in Genesis 3:15. The price for the sins of humanity was paid by Jesus Christ! God's plan to redeem humanity was set in motion on that very day sin first entered the Garden! The curse of sin, which Adam and Eve committed by disobeying God in the Garden, separated us from God in that we were no longer able to be in his presence. After they sinned, the Lord sacrificed an animal to cover Adam and Eve's nakedness or sin. This set in motion God's requirement of an animal blood sacrifice to cover the sin of man. For those of us who believe in Jesus, His crucifixion was the final blood sacrifice of atonement that would ever be required to reconcile man back to God.

> *Hebrews 9:22 – 22 And almost all things are by the law purged with blood; and without shedding of blood is no remission [forgiveness, deliverance, liberty]*

Notice the above scripture said "almost" all things are purified by the shedding of blood. It was a general custom in the Old Testament to purify everything by blood. This rule was not universal, as some things were purified by fire and water. (See Numbers 31:23.) Other things were purified by water only. (See Numbers 31:24; Leviticus 16:26-28.) But the exceptions to the general rule were few. Almost everything in the tabernacle and temple service was consecrated or purified by blood. The fullness of the meaning is that there is no forgiveness, deliverance, or liberty/freedom from sin without the shedding of blood.

There are many examples in the Old Testament alluding to the blood of the lamb. Let's look at some of these scriptural examples:

> *Genesis 4:2, 4 - 2 And she again bare his brother Abel. And Abel was a keeper of sheep, but Cain was a tiller of the ground. ... 4 And Abel, he also brought of the firstlings of his flock and of the fat thereof. And the LORD had respect unto Abel and to his offering:*

This may be the first scripture that shows a lamb being sacrificed. The blood of this lamb was honored or respected by God.

> *Exodus 12:21-23 - 21 Then Moses called for all the elders of Israel, and said unto them, Draw out and take you a lamb according to your families, and kill the passover. 22 And ye shall take a bunch of hyssop, and dip [it] in the blood that [is] in the bason, and strike the lintel and the two side posts with the blood that [is] in the bason; and none of you shall go out at the door of his house until the morning. 23 For the LORD will pass through to smite the Egyptians; and when he seeth the blood upon the lintel, and on the two side posts, the LORD will pass*

> *over the door, and will not suffer*
> *the destroyer to come in unto your*
> *houses to smite [you].*

This scripture in Exodus truly exemplifies what was to come at the cross. The children of Israel who were held in captivity in Egypt were saved or covered by the blood of the lamb on their door post. It covered them so that the destroyer passed by them and they didn't suffer the anger or wrath of God.

Old Testament stories are types and shadows of what was to come. What was, will be! Because of the Lord's crucifixion on the cross, we as God's children are now covered by the blood of the perfect Lamb of God.

> *John 29 says it quite clearly, 'The*
> *next day John saw Jesus coming*
> *toward him, and said, "Behold,*
> *the Lamb of God who takes away*
> *the sin of the world!"*

Notice this scripture said, "who **takes away** the sin of the world." Jesus was the **only** perfect sacrifice who could take away our sin. Any other blood sacrifice could only cover the sin, not take it away.

This means that in the same way that the Israelites who were covered by the blood of the Passover lamb during the exodus were spared from God's wrath, we as believers in Jesus will not suffer the wrath of God that is yet to come at the end of the age.

> *1 Thessalonians 5:9-10 - 9 For God hath not appointed us to wrath, but to obtain salvation by our Lord Jesus Christ, 10 Who died for us, that, whether we wake or sleep, we should live together with him.*

FINAL SLIDE IMAGE:

Picture of the crucified Christ with John 3:16 written next to it.

> *John 3:16 – 16 For God so loved the world, that he gave his only begotten Son, that whosoever believeth in him should not perish, but have everlasting life.*

We really need to understand the significance of what Jesus, who was God enrobed in flesh, did for us on that cross! It all started in the Garden when Adam and Eve disobeyed God.

Mankind spiritually died there and we were separated from God because of our sin.

On that day when the veil was torn in two, in that moment, God provided a way for us to be reconnected back to Him! The blood shed on that cross by the perfect Lamb of God was the **only** thing that could reverse what happened in the Garden! We can now be forgiven of our sin and approach the throne of God! God fixed what happened in the Garden! Today! We have this today!

So, why did God do this for us? Because it is God's desire that no one would be lost. God gave his only begotten Son so we might have eternal life. What was the purpose of the crucifixion of the only begotten Son of God? The purpose was this: Only the blood of the perfect Lamb of God could reverse the curse of the sin of man that originated back in the Garden of Eden! Because of Jesus' sacrifice on that cross, sin no longer has power over us, and we can be reconnected back to God!

The veil has been torn, and God is here waiting for you. Repent! God doesn't want you lost or to suffer His wrath. Hell is not God's desire for you! Come to Christ! Please don't hesitate! You do not know if you have tomorrow. Repent, and be covered by the blood of the Lamb! God provided the way back to Him so we could have eternal life with Him, but that choice is yours to make.

NOTES FROM CATHERINE:

This segment of this sermon series opened my eyes as to why Jesus had to die that horrible death so my/our sins could be forgiven! I never was able to connect the dots between the Old Testament and the New Testament on my own!

The **only** perfect sacrifice that could ultimately and finally forgive the sins of man would be a blood sacrifice of a perfect man. Since there is no such thing as a perfect human being, **only** God enrobed in flesh could be that perfect and ultimate sacrifice for the forgiveness and eradication of our sins. God is perfect. Jesus was God in the flesh, the only begotten Son of the Father. He alone could save us from our sins through the shedding of His blood to reverse what happened in the Garden in order to reconcile us back to Him! And consider that He suffered and died for us knowingly, intentionally, and willingly!!

Praise the Lord for all He has done for us!

HE HAS RISEN

PRE-SERMON VIDEO:

Picture the Garden of Gethsemane where our Lord sweat drops of blood in prayer. The following words appear:

> ALTHOUGH HE WAS BETRAYED,
> HIS PLANS WERE FULFILLED.

Next, we see a stump with a whip laid across it and these words appear:

> THOUGH THEY BEAT HIM MERCILESSLY,
> HIS MERCY ONLY MAGNIFIED.

Then, we see the cross and these words appear:

> THOUGH HE WAS MOCKED UPON THE CROSS,
> HE FORGAVE EVERY TRESPASS.

A blank gray screen displays as a veil that is torn, and these words appear:

> THOUGH GOD'S PRESENCE WAS FORBIDDEN,
> THE SACRIFICE TORE THE VEIL ASUNDER.

Next, we see a dead body wrapped in white cloth resting on a huge flat stone in a darkened grave sepulcher, and the following words appear:

THOUGH HE WAS SHROUDED IN GRAVE CLOTHES,
HIS LIGHT COULD NOT BE CONTAINED.

The grave clothes collapse flat into the stone, the music swells, and the stone of the grave is rolled away to let light into the darkened grave as these words appear:

AND THOUGH THEY SEALED HIS TOMB,
HE BROKE FREE. HE IS ALIVE! HE IS RISEN!
DEATH HAS NO VICTORY! DEATH HAS NO STING!
HIS GRACE IS TRIUMPHANT!

Finally, we see three crosses of Calvary at sunrise with the following words displayed:

GLORIFY THE NAME OF JESUS!
OUR KING FOREVER!

OPENING SLIDE:

A picture of the empty cross of Christ atop a hill with these words: "HE HAS RISEN. Death, where is your sting?"

The Sermon:

Resurrection Sunday is the day that most people refer to as Easter. I prefer to call it Resurrection Sunday because it is a better reflection of the day on which we celebrate Christ's victory over sin and death through the cross and His resurrection. It is the fulfillment of that which was promised by God in the Garden of Eden, a covenant which couldn't be broken, a path to restore man from his fallen state in order for us to be reconnected back to God. It is such a very special day! It is a day that should **not** be marred by the traditions of man that we see today, such as chocolate eggs and easter bunnies. Resurrection Sunday should be celebrated as a day in which Jesus Christ defeated death and triumphed in victory over the forces of evil!

> *Luke 18:31-34 - 31 Then he [Jesus] took [unto him] the twelve, and said unto them, Behold, we go up to Jerusalem, and all things that are written by the prophets concerning the Son of man shall be accomplished. 32 For he shall be delivered unto the Gentiles, and shall be mocked, and spitefully entreated, and spitted*

on: 33 And they shall scourge [him], and put him to death: and the third day he shall rise again. 34 And they understood none of these things: and this saying was hid from them, neither knew they the things which were spoken.

In this scripture, the word "hid" means that the apostles could not comprehend the meaning of the Lord's words. They could not understand His message because the Lord's words did not fit their narrative or expectations. They believed that Jesus was the Messiah who would lead them to victory over the oppressors of Israel, but Jesus was letting them know otherwise and they could not fathom it.

In the same way today, the words written in the Book of Revelation do not fit most people's agendas. Therefore, they don't believe it, and they do not want to believe it! Let us not be that way! Let us understand that only truth is written about in the Bible.

Luke 24:1-11 - 1 Now upon the first [day] of the week, very early in the morning, they came unto the sepulchre, bringing the spices which they had prepared, and certain [others] with them. 2 And they found the stone rolled away from the sepulchre. 3 And they entered in, and found not the body of the Lord Jesus. 4 And it came to pass, as they were much perplexed thereabout, behold, two men stood by them in shining garments: 5 And as they were afraid, and bowed down [their] faces to the earth, they said unto them, Why seek ye the living among the dead? 6 He is not here, but is risen: remember how he spake unto you when he was yet in Galilee, 7 Saying, The Son of man must be delivered into the hands of sinful men, and be crucified, and the third day rise again. 8 And they remembered his words, 9 And returned from the sepulchre, and told all these things unto the eleven, and to all the rest. 10 It was Mary Magdalene, and Joanna, and Mary [the mother] of James, and other [women that were] with them, which told these things unto the apostles. 11 And their words seemed to them as idle tales, and they believed them not.

I ponder what it must have been like for the apostles and those with them. They had walked with Jesus, dined with Jesus, and had seen the miracles done by Jesus. But now to their understanding, He was dead. The Bible said they were mourning and weeping with such grief. The sadness, fear, and doubt must have totally gripped them. They must have lost all faith as their hopes were crushed by the crucifixion and death of the One they thought was the Christ, meaning the long-awaited Messiah.

But why did the apostles have such sadness and fear? Jesus had told them on several occasions that He was going to be crucified, die, and days later be resurrected from the dead. But as the scripture said, they couldn't understand in their own minds what Jesus was telling them. They had a false perception of the Messiah and His purpose in His first coming. Messiah Jesus had come the first time to conquer the wages of sin and death, not to conquer the kingdoms of this world.

The question today is do we really understand the crucifixion and resurrection?

Too many in the world today view the resurrection as a fairy tale, or great story made up by men who were delusional. But what is fascinating is that the resurrection can be established and verified by **historical** evidence outside the Bible.

> *1 Corinthians 15:12-14 - 12 Now if Christ be preached that he rose from the dead, how say some among you that there is no resurrection of the dead? 13 But if there be no resurrection of the dead, then is Christ not risen: 14 And if Christ be not risen, then [is] our preaching vain, and your faith [is] also vain.*

In his letter to the Church in Corinth, the Apostle Paul is saying that there were some who were claiming falsely that there is no resurrection from the dead. But Paul asserted that the resurrection of Jesus from the dead is proof that there is resurrection, and that Christ's resurrection is also the promise to us who believe in Him that we will also rise from the dead at the end of the age. But Paul goes on to testify that since countless people witnessed Jesus alive after He was resurrected from the dead, we can have confidence that there is a resurrection and that we who believe in Jesus will be resurrected to eternal life to spend eternity with the Lord just as He promised.

> *1 Corinthians 15:20-22 - 20 But now*

> is Christ risen from the dead, [and]
> become the first fruits of them that
> slept. 21 For since by man [came]
> death, by man [came] also the
> resurrection of the dead. 22 For as
> in Adam all die, even so in Christ
> shall all be made alive.

If God had not intervened as He did, man was destined to be separated from God for all eternity. This was not the will of God! Praise God for having a plan for our redemption!

> 1 Corinthians 15:55-57 - 55 O
> death, where [is] thy sting? O
> grave, where [is] thy victory? 56
> The sting of death [is] sin; and the
> strength of sin [is] the law. 57 But
> thanks [be] to God, which giveth
> us the victory through our Lord
> Jesus Christ.

Because of the resurrection of Christ Jesus, death was defeated!

Let's go back and take a look at what we have learned thus far in this series. The first sin of man happened in the Garden of Eden and in that day, man died spiritually, was separated from God, and now would fall victim to physical death. But thank God, He had a plan to correct everything that went wrong in the Garden. God's only begotten Son, Jesus, came to earth to be that perfect sacrifice that would allow for our sins to be forgiven. His shed blood on the cross was that perfect sacrifice! The crucifixion provided the way for our sins to be forgiven. The resurrection of Jesus from the dead overcame death so that we, too, could have eternal life.

FINAL SLIDE IMAGE:

Picture of Mary peering through the empty tomb with the risen Jesus standing behind her and the words display: "HE is RISEN. He died so we might live."

Come to Jesus now! Through the crucifixion and resurrection from the dead, Jesus overcame death. My physical body is appointed to die once, but as a Spirit-filled follower of Jesus, I am going to be raised from the dead! Thank you, Jesus! Amen!

To those reading this, just like Adam was asked, I ask you now: "Where are you?" Jesus made a way for you to be reconnected back to God, and He went to the cross for you so you could be forgiven, and He overcame death so that you might live! Jesus is saying that He took care of our problem and provided the way to be reconnected back to God for all eternity. He is asking you now, "Where are you?"

But here's the thing: it is your choice! It's your choice whether or not you will follow Jesus. You don't know if you have tomorrow or even the next ten minutes. Please don't wait! The gift of salvation is waiting for you now!

I was once asked by someone, "What is the difference between Christianity and all the other religions? Don't they all worship the same God or higher power?" My response to this person was, "In how many of those faiths that worship a god did their god suffer and die for them? Other than Jesus Christ, NONE!" Think about that. There are not multiple ways to God, salvation, and eternal life. Jesus said, "I am the way, the truth, and the life. No one comes to the Father except through Me!" (See John 14:6.) Please grasp this!

Again, not one of us is guaranteed tomorrow. It is only through Christ Jesus that there is forgiveness of sin, eternal life, and salvation or a reconnection back to God!

NOTES FROM CATHERINE:

In re-reading and re-listening to George's sermon for Resurrection Sunday, it brought to mind a book that I read years ago called *The Case for Christ* by Lee Strobel. In this book, the author set out to disprove Christianity and Jesus. But instead, his studies led him to faith in Jesus and the Gospel. One of the many things written in that book that I recall was that all but one of the twelve apostles of Jesus willingly died horrific deaths as a martyr for Christ. None of them renounced their faith in the face of extreme suffering and brutality which resulted in their deaths. Strobel's point was that there is absolutely nobody on the planet who would willingly suffer and die for a lie! Jesus is the way, the truth and the life!

SPIRITUALLY RECONNECTED BACK TO GOD

PRE-SERMON VIDEO:

Picture flames of fire burning behind the words:

PENTECOST:
SPIRITUALLY RECONNECTED BACK TO GOD

This fades to a black background which shows the words:

WHEN THE DAY OF PENTECOST CAME,
THEY WERE ALL GATHERED TOGETHER IN ONE PLACE.

The background music increases in volume and these words appear:

SUDDENLY
A SOUND LIKE THE BLOWING OF A VIOLENT WIND
CAME FROM HEAVEN.

Then, the entire background fills with flames and these words appear:

AND FILLED THE WHOLE HOUSE
WHERE THEY WERE SITTING.
THEY SAW WHAT SEEMED TO BE
TONGUES OF FIRE THAT SEPARATED
AND CAME TO REST ON EACH OF THEM.

Then, a large ball of fire burst on the screen, followed by these words:

ALL OF THEM WERE FILLED WITH THE HOLY SPIRIT AND BEGAN TO SPEAK IN OTHER TONGUES AS THE SPIRIT ENABLED THEM. — ACTS 2:1-4.

THE SERMON:

Christians celebrate Pentecost which is the outpouring of the Holy Spirit, which enables us who believe Jesus to be filled with the Holy Spirit. Without God's Spirit living inside of us, we have no hope for salvation and being reconnected back to God, and we have no hope of reversing the curse of sin of man going all the way back to the Garden!

I would like to give a quick review of what happened in the Garden of Eden:

1. The sin committed by Adam and Eve condemned man.

2. Man experienced a sudden spiritual death.

3. We were now separated from God.

4. We would now die physically and our bodies would return to dust.

In other words, we were lost and doomed. Man would now suffer physical death as well as an eternal separation from God unless God chose to intervene on our behalf. Give all honor and praise to God for He had a plan for our redemption!

> *Genesis 3:15 - 15 And I will put enmity between thee and the woman, and between thy seed and her seed; it shall bruise thy head, and thou shalt bruise his heel.*

This was God's promise and plan for our redemption, and God always keeps His promises! Without God's promise and plan stated in this scripture, we literally have nothing! But this was actually more than a promise. It was a covenant! A covenant is always sealed by blood.

> *John 1:1, 14 - 1 In the beginning was the Word, and the Word was with God, and the Word was God. ... 14 And the Word was made flesh, and dwelt among us, (and we beheld his glory, the glory as of the only begotten of the Father,) full of grace and truth.*

This tells us that Jesus was present with God from the beginning. Only Jesus, the spotless Lamb of God, could be the perfect blood sacrifice to seal the covenant and pay for the atonement and forgiveness of mankind's sins. Jesus, the perfect sacrifice, was there from the very beginning to undo what had been done by man's sin in the Garden!

Romans 5 tells us that by one man's sin (Adam) we were condemned, and by one man's righteousness (Jesus) we were justified and saved. But how would He do this?

THE CROSS

> *John 3:14-15 - 14 And as Moses lifted up the serpent in the wilderness, even so must the Son of man be lifted up: 15 That whosoever believeth in him should not perish, but have eternal life.*

In this scripture, Jesus is referring to a time in the Old Testament when Moses lifted up a bronze serpent hanging on a cross for the Israelites in the wilderness. Due to the rebellion of the Israelites against God, God had sent fiery serpents to sting and kill them. But when the Israelites who had been bitten by the serpents looked up in faith to the cross which Moses held up, they would be restored to full health instead of dying. This was a foreshadow of the crucifixion and resurrection of Christ because those who look in faith to the cross of Christ Jesus will be healed of their sin and saved from death!

Jesus was the perfect, unblemished sacrificial Lamb whose spilled blood on the cross has overcome the sin of man in the Garden. Sin no longer has dominion over us, and because of this, we can be reconnected back to God! Jesus' blood on the cross crushed Satan's head once and for all!

Jesus' blood and death on the cross paid the ultimate price required to free man (us) from sin and spiritual death and to reverse our separation from God. Jesus' resurrection from the dead overcame physical death so that those with faith in Christ can have eternal life with Him!

THE RESURRECTION

> *Luke 24:3-6a - 3 And they entered in, and found not the body of the Lord Jesus. 4 And it came to pass, as they were much perplexed thereabout, behold, two men stood by them in shining garments: 5 And as they were afraid, and bowed down [their] faces to the earth, they said unto them, Why seek ye the living among the dead? 6a He is not here, but is risen!*

81

1 Peter 1:3 - 3 Blessed [be] the God and Father of our Lord Jesus Christ, which according to his abundant mercy hath begotten us again unto a lively hope by the resurrection of Jesus Christ from the dead,

This means that death and the grave have no more dominion over us! In Hebrew, the word spirit (ruah, pronounced roo'-akh) means the breath or wind of God! God breathed life into Adam. Jesus breathed on the apostles to receive the Holy Spirit. Then on the day of Pentecost, the breath of God came in the form of a mighty rushing wind (ruah) and enveloped and filled the disciples of Jesus with God's Spirit (ruah!).

PENTECOST

Acts 2:1-4 - 1 And when the day of Pentecost was fully come, they were all with one accord in one place. 2 And suddenly there came a sound from heaven as of a rushing mighty wind, and it filled all the house where they were sitting. 3 And there appeared unto them cloven tongues like as of fire, and it sat upon each of them. 4 And they were all filled

with the Holy Ghost, and began to
speak with other tongues, as the
Spirit gave them utterance.

Remember that when man first sinned in the Garden, he died spiritually and was separated from God. Pentecost, which depicts the infilling of the Holy Spirit, denotes our spiritual RE-birth and reconnection back to God. This is the final step in God's plan to reverse the curse that befell man in the Garden.

But also, in Acts 2:38 Peter stated that we must **repent** first and be baptized in the name of Jesus Christ in order to be cleansed so that we can be filled with the Holy Spirit of the living God! Repentance is so much more than a flippant "I'm sorry." Repentance means a change of mind, a change of heart, and a turning away from sin. Baptism involves a public declaration of our intentions to fully follow and obey Jesus Christ and proclaim the truth of the Gospel message.

PETER'S FIRST SERMON

Acts 2:17-21 - 17 And it shall come
to pass in the last days, saith God, I
will pour out of my Spirit upon all
flesh: and your sons and your
daughters shall prophesy, and

your young men shall see visions, and your old men shall dream dreams: 18 And on my servants and on my handmaidens I will pour out in those days of my Spirit; and they shall prophesy: 19 And I will shew wonders in heaven above, and signs in the earth beneath; blood, and fire, and vapour of smoke: 20 The sun shall be turned into darkness, and the moon into blood, before that great and notable day of the Lord come: 21 And it shall come to pass, [that] whosoever shall call on the name of the Lord shall be saved.

This is the final fulfillment of the promise from Genesis 3:15 of being spiritually born again and reconnected back to God by the in-filling of the Spirit of God.

IN SUMMARY:

1. Because of the blood of the perfect Lamb of God spilled on the cross, our sins can be forgiven once and for all!

2. Because of Jesus' resurrection from the dead, the grave and death are defeated!

3. Because of the gift of the Holy Spirit, we can be reconnected back to God.

At the end of time, those who have been filled with God's Holy Spirit will find themselves in their glorified bodies residing back in the Garden with the Lord for all eternity. Praise the Lord for His provision and plan!

To state it simply, mankind had a problem but now we have God's solution:

Man's Problem	God's Solution
Sin	Crucifixion
Death	Resurrection
Separation from God	Reconnection back to God through the Holy Spirit

God loved us so much that He had a plan for our redemption from the very beginning! Hell was never created for man. It was created for the angels that rebelled and sinned against God. But since sinful man would suffer the same eternal fate as the fallen angels, God made a way for our escape. Please take advantage of the plan of God for He would have it that none be lost!

Do you realize that Spirit filled followers of Christ will spend eternity walking and talking with Jesus in the Garden just as God had always intended? There will be no more death and no more sorrow there! What can the world possibly offer you that would be better than that? There is nothing the world can offer that even begins to compare to that!

How can anyone be more enamored of a newer, bigger house that will decay someday than eternal life spent with the Lord? The Bible says that where your treasure is, there your heart will be also. If your treasures and heart are with this world and the things of this world, then you will perish with the world also. If your treasure and heart is with the Lord, then you will live with the Lord for all eternity.

FINAL SLIDE IMAGE:

Picture the crucified Christ on the cross with these words: "Everything that happened in the Garden has been nullified! God has made a way for us to return to Him. He is waiting for you!"

God is waiting for you to choose Him. Just like He said to Adam, "Where are you? I've made a way for you to be with me for all eternity." All you have to do is say, "Here I am, Lord," and truly repent, and serve Him with all your heart and substance. What do you get in return? You get to walk with Jesus on streets of gold for all eternity!

This opportunity will not last forever. Just as in the days of Noah when God's hand shut the door to the ark just prior to His wrath being poured out on the earth, this period of God's grace will also come to an end. Since no one knows the day or hour of the Lord's return which will herald the end of this age of grace, I beg you to choose wisely and choose now whom you will serve!

NOTES FROM CATHERINE:

There you have it! The who, what, when, where, how, and why of the Gospel story of our Lord and Savior Christ Jesus! It tells us of the unfathomable and undeserved love our marvelous Creator has for us!

Section 3:

The Foundation for the Christian Life

This section of the book contains teachings based on sermon notes and videos of sermons that George prepared, used, and taught at various times. He purposefully set them aside for inclusion in this book to help all believers have the right foundation for living their lives for God until Jesus returns.

Are You the Light?

Picture a single light bulb, turned off, and hanging in a darkened room, which then turns on and lights up. Soft music is playing in the background. These words appear:

THIS IS YOUR LIGHT
AND YOUR LIGHT SPREADS GOD'S LOVE.
WITHOUT IT, YOU ARE IN COMPLETE DARKNESS.

The next scene contains several light bulbs, also turned off, swirling around the first light bulb that is now lit up. The music increases slightly in volume and strength. These words appear:

LET YOUR LIGHT SHINE AMONG MEN, THAT THEY MAY
SEE YOUR GOOD DEEDS AND GLORIFY YOUR FATHER.

YOUR LIGHT CAN DO GREAT THINGS.

One by one, the darkened light bulbs become lit as they continue to swirl around the original light bulb. The music increases more in volume and strength. These words appear:

YOUR LIGHT CAN INSPIRE OTHERS,
REACH THE LOST, CHANGE LIVES, LOVE.
WITHOUT IT, WE WOULD ALL BE LOST IN THE DARKNESS.
SO SHINE GOD'S LOVE FOR THE WORLD TO SEE.

The music crescendos, and the video ends.

THE SERMON:

What is the light? In order to be the light, we must first understand what the light is. We know from scripture that Jesus was the light unto all men.

> *John 1:1-5 - 1 In the beginning was the Word, and the Word was with God, and the Word was God. 2 The same was in the beginning with God. 3 All things were made by him; and without him was not anything made that was made. 4 In him was life; and the life was the light of men. 5 And the light shineth in darkness; and the darkness comprehended it not.*

The Word of God represents the will, nature, and character of God. The Word was with God before anything was created. The Word is eternal. It has always been. It has no beginning and no end. The life in Jesus was the absolute fullness of the life of God dwelling in Him. That life was the essence of God and all that He is shining like a light through the person of Jesus. Jesus was the Word, meaning the will, nature, and character of God enrobed in flesh.

In the Greek, the word light is derived from *phos*. When Jesus was called the Light, He was being called the *Phos*. In the natural, *phos* means light as emitted from a lamp. Metaphorically and spiritually, *phos* means the power of understanding moral and spiritual truths. In other words, to know the truth. We know the saying that the truth will set you free, but first we must see the truth through the light. Jesus is that Light!

In this scripture, when it says that the Light shines in the darkness and the darkness did not comprehend it, it is referring to the fact that Jesus, the Light, came to this world that is overrun by the evil one and was rejected by the world because the world did not understand who He was. He even stood right in front of the religious leaders, the Sadducees and Pharisees who knew the Word of God as the Holy Scriptures, but even they could not perceive that standing right in front of them was the Word of God enrobed in flesh! Everything Jesus said and did was darkness to them because they were in darkness.

> *John 1:10-13 - 10 He was in the world, and the world was made by him, and the world knew him not. 11 He came unto his own, and his own received him not. 12 But as many as received him, to them gave he power to become the sons of God, [even] to them that believe on his name: 13 Which were born, not of blood, nor of the will of the flesh, nor of the will of man, but of God.*

What this scripture means is that those who believe in Jesus and have been filled with His Holy Spirit have been born again, not born of the corruptible seed of man, meaning their biological ancestry through their parents, but born of the incorruptible seed of the Spirit of the living God. They have been given power, meaning authority, from God to become His children.

> *John 3:6 - 6 That which is born of the flesh is flesh; and that which is born of the Spirit is spirit.*

In this scripture, when Jesus speaks about being born again, He is referring to a spiritual re-birth through the incorruptible seed of God's Holy Spirit. In order to be born again spiritually, one must believe that Jesus is the Son of God, acknowledge their own inherent sinful nature, ask God for forgiveness for their sins, and repent by turning away from sin. Then, we must invite God to be the Lord of our lives by inviting His Holy Spirit to dwell within us to be our King. This leads to a personal relationship with Christ Jesus and is the start of being born again by God's Spirit!

Jesus is the Word (or total essence) of God enrobed in flesh. The Word of God is the Light! When we become "born-again" and are filled with God's Holy Spirit, or God's essence, we become the word of God or light unto men. We are no longer living in the flesh but have become a new creature in Christ, because we have been spiritually born again. The Word of God has been written on the tables of our heart as prophesied.

> Jeremiah 31:33 - 33 But this [shall be] the covenant that I will make with the house of Israel; After those days, saith the LORD, I will put my law in their inward parts, and write it in their hearts; and will be their God, and they shall be my people.

So, what does all this have to do with us becoming the light?

The Word of God, or God's essence, is now a living, breathing, spiritual manifestation in those of us filled with God's Holy Spirit, which means that it is no longer just words written in the pages of a book. Once we are born again and are filled with God's Holy Spirit, we become the light of God unto the world! We are not of the world anymore as we are now spiritual beings. Our hearts and minds are focused on heavenly things with the Lord, not on earthly things, when we become filled with God's Holy Spirit.

> *Matthew 5:14-16 - 14 Ye are the light of the world. A city that is set on an hill cannot be hid. 15 Neither do men light a candle, and put it under a bushel, but on a candlestick; and it giveth light unto all that are in the house. 16 Let your light so shine before men, that they may see your good works, and glorify your Father which is in heaven.*

But many say "How can this be? How can we be the light? It can't be done!" Well, here is a little secret:

> *John 6:53-54 - 53 Then Jesus said unto them, Verily, verily, I say unto you, Except ye eat the flesh of the Son of man, and drink his blood, ye have no life in you. 54 Whoso eateth my flesh, and drinketh my blood, hath eternal life; and I will raise him up at the last day.*

John already told us what the flesh is! In the beginning was the Word, and the Word was with God, and the Word became flesh and was the light unto all men. Metaphorically speaking, we know we must 'eat' the Word of God, meaning to read, study, and know it for ourselves. So, to eat Jesus is to eat the Word of God! But now, Jesus is saying that we must drink his blood. This is hard for many people to understand. From the Old Testament, we know that the blood is what gives life to the natural body, and it is considered sacred in God's sight. So now, through drinking Jesus, we have the life of God in us.

Moreover, remember, the woman at the well to whom Jesus said that He had the living water with which she would never thirst again? (See John Chapter 4.) We would be wise to ask, "What is it that is the living water that gives us life that we need to drink?" It is the Holy Spirit of the living God!

Accordingly, if you will drink the Spirit, meaning invite God's Holy Spirit to dwell within you, and eat (read) the Word daily, you WILL be that light to an otherwise dark world! What you consume daily will be put in your heart and mind, and YOU will be that light in the darkness! With so many people lost, we have an opportunity to be the light and the hope that this dark world needs!

What does all of this mean? First of all, it calls us to examine ourselves. The main questions we need to ask ourselves is this: "Am I really born-again? Am I filled with God's Holy Spirit? Am I really one of God's children?" We can only be the light if we are born-again and are filled with God's Holy Spirit. The Bible says you will know them by their fruits. The fruits of the spirit are love, joy, peace, patience/long suffering, kindness, generosity, faithfulness, gentleness, and self-control. Do you display the fruits of the Spirit?

Matthew 7 clearly states that a born-again believer in Christ will OBEY and DO the will of the Father in Heaven. A born-again believer's mind and heart will be set on the things of God, not the things of the world.

We need to ask ourselves: are we fully obedient to the Word of God in the Bible, plus to any specific directives He gives to us individually? If we continue in known sin, we cannot be the light nor can we comprehend the light, meaning that we are blind to the things of God.

> Ephesians 5:8 - 8 For ye were sometimes darkness, but now [are ye] light in the Lord: walk as children of light:

Walking as children of the Light means that we no longer follow and act upon the desires of our flesh as those of the world do. Rather, we choose to follow and obey the living God! As children of the Light, our behavior should be dramatically different from those who are of the world and do not follow Christ.

How should our behavior be different as born-again followers of Christ? The focus of those of the world tends to be very centered on themselves. Their actions are always focused on their own best benefit and pleasing themselves. Contrary to this, the actions of born-again followers of Christ are focused on pleasing the Lord and serving others for the Lord. One predominantly *takes*; the other predominantly *gives*.

I hope and I pray that this message gets ahold of you so that you can become all that you are truly meant to be in God. Only those who are in Christ Jesus and are spiritually alive and filled with God's Holy Spirit can walk in and be the light. And those of us who are already born-again must let our lights shine into this dark world with good works that are of the Spirit, not of the flesh, with the ultimate goal of bringing others to Christ and glorifying the Father in Heaven.

If you are living for God, you will know because His Spirit lives inside of you. And if you are not filled with God's Holy Spirit, then I invite you to fall on your knees and call out to the name of Jesus. He is here for you, He died on a cross for you so that you can be saved. There is no greater example of the Lord's love than what He suffered on that cross for each and every one of us!

Are you truly a born-again follower of Jesus Christ? Are you shining as the light in this world?

Is Grace the Right to Sin?

The Sermon:

In today's society and many contemporary churches, those who profess to be Christians have the opinion that we are free to remain in sin because they say, "God's grace covers us." They contend that the New Covenant did away with the moral Law of the Old Testament. Many of them come to the conclusion that we are no longer subjected to the Law or Commandments because Christ fulfilled it at the cross. Many of them say things like, "God understands that humans are not perfect and, therefore, does not expect humans to live a holy life." Unfortunately, they take scriptures out of context to justify error.

While we know that God is merciful and that Jesus died on a cross for our sins, we must ask ourselves if this perspective that the grace of God permits us to continue in sin is biblically true. We need to look at what the Word of God has to say about this, especially since the choices we make on this earth will determine our eternal destiny – in Heaven with the Lord, or in Hell.

Let's look at one of the more popular scriptures

that is used out of context to justify continued sin:

> *Romans 3:23 - 23 For all have sinned, and come short of the glory of God;*

Nowhere and in no way does Romans 3:23 imply that once you know the truth and are saved, you are free to go out there and sin! In fact, this scripture is utilized in the **past tense** and not the present or future tense! Our inherent nature **prior** to being filled with God's Holy Spirit is sinful, and in that sense, all have sinned and fall short of the glory of God.

When the woman caught in the act of adultery was brought before Jesus, the people were going to stone her to death in accordance with the Law's penalty for her behavior. When Jesus called for those without sin to be the first to throw a stone against her, all of her accusers left. Then, Jesus asked her who was still standing there to condemn her.

> *John 8:11 - 11 She said, No man, Lord. And Jesus said unto her, Neither do I condemn thee: go, and sin no more.*

It is clear from this scripture that Jesus told this woman caught in the act of sinning, to **stop** doing it. His words were, "Go and sin **no more**!" And Jesus meant **no more**. Jesus is saying that He forgave her of her sin, then follows up with a command (not a suggestion) to **stop** doing it. Now, we have to remember that if the Lord tells us to stop doing something, or to do something in particular, He will enable us to do so! Jesus was not sent to condemn her or us. Rather, Jesus was sent to deliver her and us from our sin!

> *Hebrews 10:26, 29 - 26 For if we sin wilfully after that we have received the knowledge of the truth, there remaineth no more sacrifice for sins, ... 29 Of how much sorer punishment, suppose ye, shall he be thought worthy, who hath trodden under foot the Son of God, and hath counted the blood of the covenant, wherewith he was sanctified, an unholy thing, and hath done despite unto the Spirit of grace?*

These scriptures refer to someone who once accepted Christ, but later goes on to continue in a life of sin. If they remain in this sinful state of apostasy against the Lord, there is no hope for the forgiveness of their sin, and they can no longer be reconciled back to God. The word used in this passage to say that they have *troddened* the Son of God means that they have heartlessly shown indifference to Jesus through their actions.

There is a huge difference between intentional sin versus unintentional sin. Unintentional sin is sin without the knowledge that the act is sinful. It is done in ignorance of God's Word and ways. But once we are filled with God's Holy Spirit, the Spirit inside of us will convict us of what is sinful. And as Spirit filled believers, what are we supposed to do when we are convicted of sin? We must repent! To repent means to change our minds and turn away from (or stop doing) that sin!

When we knowingly, intentionally sin after we have been filled with God's Holy Spirit, we actually insult and mock the Holy Spirit of the one true living God.

> *1 John 3:6-10 - 6 Whosoever abideth in him sinneth not: whosoever sinneth hath not seen him, neither known him. 7 Little children, let no man deceive you: he that doeth righteousness is righteous, even as he is righteous. 8 He that committeth sin is of the devil; for the devil sinneth from the*

beginning. For this purpose the Son of God was manifested, that he might destroy the works of the devil. 9 Whosoever is born of God doth not commit sin; for his seed remaineth in him: and he cannot sin, because he is born of God. 10 In this the children of God are manifest, and the children of the devil: whosoever doeth not righteousness is not of God, neither he that loveth not his brother.

When you practice something, you intentionally plan and do it! Anyone who is truly saved by God does **not** repetitively commit the same known sin! As fallible human beings, we will sometimes unintentionally sin and mess up, but we **do not plan** it out in our head! We **do not practice** it!! According to this scripture, the one who intentionally plans and commits a known sin, especially repeatedly, is of the devil and has not been born again of God! This scripture makes plain that Jesus came to **destroy** the works of the devil, not to permit them! We can be delivered of sin once we are filled with God's Holy Spirit. The Bible is a book of **victory** for the faithful not a book of defeat!

Romans 3:31 - 31 Do we then make void [nullify, do away with]

> *the law [that which pertains to the divine will of God] through faith? God forbid: yea, we establish [affirm] the law.*

This scripture is asking if having faith in God allows us to destroy the divine will of God or His Word? Emphatically, the answer is **absolutely not**! Because we have faith in God, we uphold the Word and divine will of God and affirm it through our lives. Faith does **not** nullify or destroy the Law, but it is through faith that we uphold the Law!

> *1 Peter 1:14-16 - 14 As obedient children, not fashioning yourselves according to the former lusts in your ignorance: 15 But as he which hath called you is holy, so be ye holy in all manner of conversation [conduct]; 16 Because it is written, Be ye holy; for I am holy. (quoting Leviticus 11:44.)*

These scriptures clearly delineate that our pre-born-again nature is a sinful nature. Once we come to Christ and are born again, the Lord expects us as His children, to be obedient, righteous, and holy because He is holy. What does the word holy mean? According to Strongs G40, it means sacred, morally blameless, and consecrated before God.

Even though we are covered under the New Covenant of God's grace, the Old Covenant Law of God has not been nullified or replaced. In order to understand the full truth, we need to look at some Old Testament scriptures.

> *Hebrews 8:10 - 10 For this [is] the covenant that I will make with the house of Israel after those days, saith the Lord; I will put my laws into their mind, and write them in their hearts: and I will be to them a God, and they shall be to me a people: (Quoting Jeremiah 31:33 in the Old Testament.)*

> *Ezekiel 36:26 - 26 A new heart also will I give you, and a new spirit will I put within you: and I will take away the stony heart out of your flesh, and I will give you an heart of flesh.*

These promises were given by God to his people of the Old Testament for a time to come. This promise was fulfilled on the day of Pentecost written about in the Book of Acts. Writing His Word in our minds and hearts and placing a new Spirit within us certainly sounds like being born again! The Word of God is now **in** us, **in** our hearts and minds – not just on paper or a piece of stone anymore. If God's Word is true, how could God's grace permit us to abolish His Word once we are saved? It does not!

God writes His Word in our minds and hearts once we are born again. When my wife was very young in Christ and recently filled with God's Holy Spirit, the Lord would speak through her to give words of encouragement to her Pastor. Every time the Lord would give her a word to speak, He would have her quote a relevant scripture verbatim from the Bible as part of the message. What is very amusing to me and was also amusing to her Pastor, was that she had not yet read the Bible at that very early time of her walk with the Lord! How could this be? Because the Word of God, the Light, God's Holy Spirit was inside of her!

Spirit-filled believers no longer live under the oldness of the letter of the Law but live under the newness of the Spirit. The Word of God is now in our minds and written on our hearts! The Law went from one state to another, from flesh to Spirit, from death to life.

> *Romans 6:1-2 - 1 What shall we say then? Shall we continue in sin, that grace may abound? 2 God forbid. How shall we, that are dead to sin, live any longer therein?*

Paul was teaching that if people were not filled with the Holy Spirit, they could not overcome the flesh to stop sinning. Our flesh is at enmity with God. The written Law condemned us all in the flesh since the flesh, in and of itself, cannot perfectly obey the Law. Conversely, only those filled with God's Holy Spirit who are strengthened by His grace can overcome sin.

FINAL SLIDE IMAGE:

A picture of Christ crucified on the cross with His body limp. The words on the slide: "The question is: Did Christ die on the cross so you could live in bondage or be set free from sin?"

Don't tell me that God's grace has set you free while you are still living in bondage to sin. When you truly come to Christ, you **must** repent of your sins and stop doing them! We must ask ourselves if our lives reflect what we claim is in our heart.

> Romans 8:1-4 - 1 [There is] therefore now no condemnation to them which are in Christ Jesus, who walk not after the flesh, but after the Spirit. 2 For the law of the Spirit of life in Christ Jesus hath made me free from the law of sin and death.

3 For what the law could not do, in that it was weak through the flesh, God sending his own Son in the likeness of sinful flesh, and for sin, condemned sin in the flesh: 4 That the righteousness of the law might be fulfilled in us, who walk not after the flesh, but after the Spirit.

When people claim that it is ok to sin because they say, "God understands and His grace covers us," they are actually denying the **power** of God and His Holy Spirit! Born-again Christians are the sons and daughters of God and the bride of Christ! What an honor! We will spend eternity reconnected back to God walking in the Garden with Christ just as God had always intended. We can have victory through Christ! We should be jumping for joy!

Romans 8:5-8 - 5 For they that are after the flesh do mind the things of the flesh; but they that are after the Spirit the things of the Spirit. 6 For to be carnally minded [is] death; but to be spiritually minded [is] life and peace. 7 Because the carnal mind [is] enmity against God: for it is not subject to the law of God, neither indeed can be. 8

> *So then they that are in the flesh cannot please God.*

There is a choice to be made. You can choose to follow your flesh, which is an enemy of God, and continue to live in your sin. Or, you can choose to follow Jesus in obedience and have victory in your life over sin.

> *Romans 8:9-13 - 9 But ye are not in the flesh, but in the Spirit, if so be that the Spirit of God dwell in you. Now if any man have not the Spirit of Christ, he is none of his. 10 And if Christ [be] in you, the body [is] dead because of sin; but the Spirit [is] life because of righteousness. 11 But if the Spirit of him that raised up Jesus from the dead dwell in you, he that raised up Christ from the dead shall also quicken your mortal bodies by his Spirit that dwelleth in you. 12 Therefore, brethren, we are debtors, not to the flesh, to live after the flesh. 13 For if ye live after the flesh, ye shall die: but if ye through the Spirit do mortify the deeds of the body, ye shall live.*

We are saved by the grace of God through faith in God's Son, Jesus Christ, who overcame sin on the cross. It is through grace that we can become the children of God once we are born again and are filled with His Holy Spirit. Because of the Holy Spirit residing in us, He will lead us into a spiritual life of peace and good works. Not works of the flesh but works of the Spirit.

God neither loves nor condones evil and sin. The Bible clearly defines what God considers to be evil and sinful. Our sin separated us from God. God's unmerited love was displayed for us on the cross. He died a horrific death on that cross to pay the penalty of sin that was due us. His purpose in so doing was to free us from the bondages of sin so we could spend life eternal with Him! He did not die that horrid death so that we could continue in our sins. Those who claim to love God yet continue in sin, mock their Creator!

Jesus said in John 14:15, "If you love me, keep my commandments." If you are filled with God's Holy Spirit, you will keep the two commandments which fulfil all the Laws: The first is love the Lord God with all your heart, mind, and soul and the second is love your brother as yourself. If you keep these two commandments, you will keep all of God's commandments! The scriptures say so many times that if you love God, you will obey Him!

God's grace is *not* the right to sin but the *power*

to overcome sin through God's Holy Spirit!

Notes from Catherine:

I know George would want me to urge each and every reader to closely examine your heart and behavior to see if you are being lax about sin in your life because of God's grace. Earnestly seek the Lord in prayer and ask Him to reveal to you anything that He would want you to repent from and stop doing. Seek counsel from a mature Christian Pastor, or mature Christian brother or sister in Christ. Be honest with yourself and your person of counsel. Your eternity could be at stake!

THE DESIRES OF OUR HEART

PRE-SERMON VIDEO:

This video had piano music in the background. Then, the following phrases were brought on the screen in sequential order:

OH CHRISTIAN
WHY DO YOU SUNDAY,
YET NOTHING CHANGES ON MONDAY?

WHY DO YOU LIFT YOUR HANDS IN WORSHIP,
BUT DON'T RAISE THEM AGAIN UNTIL NEXT WEEK?

OH CHRISTIAN

WHY DO YOU NOD IN AGREEMENT WITH SCRIPTURE,
BUT THE BIBLE NEVER GETS OPENED?

WHY DO YOU COME TO THE CHURCH,
INSTEAD OF *BEING* THE CHURCH?

WHY DO YOU SIT AND ENJOY THE SERVICE,
INSTEAD OF GIVING YOUR LIFE TO SERVE?

WHY DO YOU COME AND GO,
BUT NEVER STOP TO LOVE THOSE AROUND YOU?

WHY DO YOU SAY GOD IS FIRST,
YET YOU PUT HIM LAST?

OH CHRISTIAN

YOU SAY YOU BELIEVE,
BUT YOUR ACTIONS SAY THE OPPOSITE.
YOUR LIFE LOOKS NO DIFFERENT THAN ANY OTHER

YOU THINK CHURCH IS MEANT FOR YOUR ENJOYMENT
— A LIFE OF COMFORT AND EASE —
AND GOD IS THERE TO GIVE US WHAT WE WANT.

DO YOU CARRY THE BURDENS OF THOSE AROUND YOU
OR ARE YOU THE BURDEN TO THOSE AROUND YOU?

DO YOU SPEND EVERY DAY FOR GOD'S GLORY,
OR DOES HE GET WHAT'S LEFT OVER?

OH CHRISTIAN

ARE YOU A CHRISTIAN?
DO YOU KNOW WHAT IT MEANS?

LEAVING BEHIND YOUR LIFE AND TAKING UP HIS?
AND CARRYING YOUR CROSS DAILY
AND SEEKING HIS GLORY?

DO YOU KNOW THAT THIS WAS NOT MERE SUGGESTION,
BUT THE WORK YOU HAVE BEEN CALLED TO?

IT IS NOT AN OPTION, BUT IT IS YOUR CHOICE.

OH CHRISTIAN

The Sermon:

We will be discussing today whether or not God gives us the desires of our heart. Many churches today teach that God gives us the desires of our heart. But is this scripturally true? That is what we will be looking at in today's sermon.

> *Psalm 37:3-6 - 3 Trust in the LORD, and do good; [so] shalt thou dwell in the land, and verily thou shalt be fed. 4 Delight thyself also in the LORD; and he shall give thee the desires of thine heart. 5 Commit thy way unto the LORD; trust also in him; and he shall bring [it] to pass. 6 And he shall bring forth thy righteousness as the light, and thy judgment as the noonday.*

The Hebrew word for "trust" in this scripture means a total, trusting surrender to the Lord. To do this means that we now place the will of God above our own carnal will. When we truly do this, God is the One who gives us the desires of our hearts because our hearts and desires are now fully aligned with His heart and His desires for us! This can only happen if we fully submit to the Lord, repent, and are filled with the Holy Spirit of the living God!

This scripture, taken out of context, particularly verse 4, is probably one of the most widely used verses to support what is known as the prosperity preaching of today, or the "name it and claim it" false doctrine to which so many people are drawn. False teachers distort the true meaning of God's word, teaching people who do not know any better to approach our God and Savior as little more than a cosmic vending machine made to gratify their selfish, carnal desires. The Bible says false hope makes the heart sorrowful and the result of this teaching is exactly that - many souls disillusioned and lost.

Let's look at some other scriptures about this issue for a more comprehensive understanding of what the Word of God is truly saying:

> *James 4:1-4 - 1 From whence [come] wars and fightings among you? [come they] not hence, [even] of your lusts that war in your members? 2 Ye lust, and have not: ye kill, and desire to have, and cannot obtain: ye fight and war, yet ye have not, because ye ask not. 3 Ye ask, and receive not, because ye ask amiss, that ye may consume [it] upon your lusts. 4 Ye adulterers and adulteresses, know ye not that*

*the friendship of the world is enmity
with God? whosoever therefore will
be a friend of the world is the
enemy of God.*

James clearly establishes that if we petition God for things that are of a fleshly nature and carnal desires, God will not hear us nor give it to us. God will not fulfill such requests because we ask of our own lustful desires instead of asking for that which is the will of God for us.

James goes on to say that those who love the world and the things of this world are actually enemies of God. In other words, their father is Satan. The Hebrew word for Satan means "adversary, enemy of, or one who opposes God." It's exactly what we **do not** want to be!

One question that begs to be answered here is how can these people be adulterers and adulteresses? In order to commit adultery, one must be betrothed/married to someone first. This would mean that James is referring to Christians betrothed to God who went on to betray Him by loving the things of the world more than Him.

*1 John 5:14-15 - 14 And this is the
confidence that we have in him,
that, if we ask any thing according*

> *to his will, he heareth us: 15 And if*
> *we know that he hear us,*
> *whatsoever we ask, we know that*
> *we have the petitions that we*
> *desired of him.*

Our Heavenly Father knows what is best for us! He is God and we are not. God grants our petitions which fall within His will for us and does not grant petitions which are out of His will for us, even if it might gratify our carnal, fleshly desires and make us happy in the short term. What good, loving father would give his child a cup of poison if he earnestly asked for it? This means that God does not grant us all the desires of our hearts because our human hearts are wicked and deceitful.

> *Jeremiah 17:9-10 - 9 The heart [is]*
> *deceitful above all [things], and*
> *desperately wicked: who can*
> *know it? 10 I the LORD search the*
> *heart, [I] try the reins, even to give*
> *every man according to his ways,*
> *[and] according to the fruit of his*
> *doings.*

If the Bible says the heart is deceitful above all things and desperately wicked, why on earth would I want the desires of it? Instead, we must use our hearts to trust God.

Proverbs 3:5-6 - 5 Trust in the LORD with all thine heart; and lean not unto thine own understanding. 6 In all thy ways acknowledge him, and he shall direct thy paths.

This scripture tells us that when we fully depend on the Lord without doubt, He will direct our paths and provide according to what is in our best interests.

Proverbs 14:12 - 12 There is a way which seemeth right unto a man, but the end thereof [are] the ways of death.

This scripture shows us that man without the Holy Spirit will always fulfill the desires of his flesh. Left to ourselves, we rationalize any choice we desire to make is the best choice simply because we will get what we desire out of it. But the fate of the unrepentant, sinful man is always death and an eternity separated from God.

When we were in the world, we were not of God. At that time, our hearts were full of deception and lies. After we have been forgiven, repent, and are filled with God's Holy Spirit, our eyes are opened and our hearts are cleansed. We are no longer controlled by the flesh but can now be led by the Spirit of God.

We become a new creature in Christ. We are to crucify our flesh and carnal will on a daily basis, pick up our cross, and follow Jesus.

> *Matthew 16:24-26 - 24 Then said Jesus unto his disciples, If any [man] will come after me, let him deny himself, and take up his cross, and follow me. 25 For whosoever will save his life shall lose it: and whosoever will lose his life for my sake shall find it. 26 For what is a man profited, if he shall gain the whole world, and lose his own soul? or what shall a man give in exchange for his soul?*

When we fully come to Christ and do this, the desires of our cleansed heart become His desires for us. His will becomes our will, and our thoughts become directed by the Holy Spirit instead of by our flesh. When this happens, the Lord will give us the desires of our heart because our desires are aligned with His will for us. That is the true meaning of Psalm 37:3-6!

This does not mean that we won't sometimes make mistakes or fail as we follow Christ. However, as a born-again Christian, it is never the intention of our heart to sin, be disobedient to, or betray God.

> *Proverbs 24:16 - 16 For a just [man] falleth seven times, and riseth up again: but the wicked shall fall into mischief.*

When a born-again Christian does error, sin, or fail, they are quick to stop and repent, ask the Lord for forgiveness, and then purpose in their heart not to repeat that error, sin, or failure again.

> *1 Timothy 6:6-9 - 6 But godliness with contentment is great gain. 7 For we brought nothing into [this] world, [and it is] certain we can carry nothing out. 8 And having food and raiment let us be therewith content. 9 But they that will be rich fall into temptation and a snare, and [into] many foolish and hurtful lusts, which drown men in destruction and perdition.*

When a person's focus is on the Lord and eternal life, he will be content in his present, temporary circumstances, even if he only has the necessities of life. Those who desire more than basic necessities actually desire to be rich. This desire for "more and better" is a trap set by the evil one as it sets the stage for selfishness, an elevation of the desires of self over the will of God. This draws us away from God, thus potentially sealing for us a fate of death and eternal separation from God.

> *Matthew 6:19-21 - 19 Lay not up for yourselves treasures upon earth, where moth and rust doth corrupt, and where thieves break through and steal: 20 But lay up for yourselves treasures in heaven, where neither moth nor rust doth corrupt, and where thieves do not break through nor steal: 21 For where your treasure is, there will your heart be also.*

As I was driving past a local dump, it occurred to me that everything in that dump was once a person's carnal dream. There was rotting furniture, rusted out cars, etc. Earthly treasures truly are temporary and will decay away just as this scripture states.

But what are Heavenly treasures that will last through all eternity? These are acts of kindness, charity, love, and generosity that we freely do unto others out of love for and service to our God. Our rewards will be in Heaven and dictated by the grace and will of God.

If our hearts are set on the treasures and pleasures of the earth, our rewards will be there also only to someday rot in an earthly dump. If our hearts are set on Heavenly treasures and the will of God, our rewards will be in Heaven with the Lord. Truly there is no greater reward than spending eternity with our Lord and Savior, Jesus!

> *1 Timothy 6:17-19 - 17 Charge them that are rich in this world, that they be not highminded, nor trust in uncertain riches, but in the living God, who giveth us richly all things to enjoy; 18 That they do good, that they be rich in good works, ready to distribute, willing to communicate; 19 Laying up in store for themselves a good foundation against the time to come, that they may lay hold on eternal life.*

I would say that these scriptures exemplify what it means to lay up treasures in Heaven. It is quite evident from them that when we are blessed with material resources, we are to be a blessing to others by sharing what we have. Truly, everything belongs to God, and we are to be good stewards of His resources given to us on earth.

Remember that on judgment day, we will be held accountable for what we did with God's resources! If we are born again in Christ Jesus, we are truly not of this world. Therefore, our hearts and what we consider to be treasures are not of this world either. Since God's perspective is always eternal, our perspective should also always be eternal. Then, when our hearts are aligned to the Lord's heart, God will surely give us the desires of our hearts.

It's not about you, but it is ALL about God!

So, does God give us the desires of our carnal, fleshly heart? The answer is unequivocally, NO! If you want love, joy, and a peace that surpasses all understanding, Jesus is here and waiting for you today. If you want everlasting, eternal life with God, Jesus is here waiting for you today. It will cost you everything in this world, but what you will gain in eternity with Him outshines anything you can imagine!

FINAL SLIDE IMAGE:

The crucified Christ's limp body on the cross with the following scripture:

> John 3:16-18 - 16 For God so loved the world, that he gave his only begotten Son, that whosoever believeth in him should not perish, but have everlasting life. 17 For

> *God sent not his Son into the world to condemn the world; but that the world through him might be saved. 18 He that believeth on him is not condemned: but he that believeth not is condemned already, because he hath not believed in the name of the only begotten Son of God.*

Many false teachers tend to leave off that last sentence when they post John 3:16 because they know the people will not like it. Only telling partial scriptures and/or scriptures out of context misleads the people to leave them deceived!

Jesus died on the cross for you and me, I strongly beseech you to repent of your sins right now, don't wait. You don't know if you have tomorrow! If you are in a church that teaches heresies or the Lord has shown you that you still have a love of the world, repent and ask God to forgive you and lead you to a true shepherd of His flock! Repentance is not just words, it is faith in action!

NOTES FROM CATHERINE:

Honestly, as George and I grew closer and closer

to the Lord together as well as individually, the greatest desire of our hearts became to know, love, and serve the Lord with all of our being. This should be true for every born-again Christian. What brought George and I the most joy was when we knew that we were in the process of directly serving the Lord and when we knew we were fully in His will for us.

The most important thing to both George and I is to one day hear these words from the Lord, "Well done, good and faithful servant." After hearing Him say, "Welcome home," I cannot imagine hearing anything that will bring me more joy!

WHO IS MY BROTHER OR SISTER?

THE SERMON:

"Who is my brother or sister?" is a question that Jesus asked His disciples. This is an interesting question. Countless times over the years, I have heard so many professed Christians say that everyone is our brother and sister in Christ. It is true that the Bible does say we are to be no respecter of persons, meaning we are not to treat anyone above or below another. Additionally, I will paraphrase this Bible message and summarize it as saying we are to treat everyone with kindness, consideration, and respect while always speaking the truth in love.

All this being said, does this mean every person on the planet is our brother or sister in Christ? We need to look at scripture in order to be able to answer this question correctly.

> *John 8:37-42, 44 – [Jesus Speaking]*
> *37 I know that ye are Abraham's seed; but ye seek to kill me, because my word hath no place in you. 38 I speak that which I have seen with my Father: and ye*

do that which ye have seen with your father. 39 They answered and said unto him, Abraham is our father. Jesus saith unto them, If ye were Abraham's children, ye would do the works of Abraham. 40 But now ye seek to kill me, a man that hath told you the truth, which I have heard of God: this did not Abraham. 41 Ye do the deeds of your father. Then said they to him, We be not born of fornication; we have one Father, [even] God. 42 Jesus said unto them, If God were your Father, ye would love me: for I proceeded forth and came from God; neither came I of myself, but he sent me. ... 44 Ye are of [your] father the devil, and the lusts of your father ye will do. He was a murderer from the beginning, and abode not in the truth, because there is no truth in him. When he speaketh a lie, he speaketh of his own: for he is a liar, and the father of it.

1 John 3:8 - 8 He that committeth sin is of the devil; for the devil sinneth from the beginning. For this purpose the Son of God was manifested, that he might destroy the works of the devil.

These verses show us that **not** every person is our brother or sister in Christ. Although it is true that God created every human being on planet Earth (see Psalms 139:13-16), He gives each of us free will to follow whomever we choose. There are only two choices: God or self/the world. If we choose ourselves over God, it actually means that we have chosen to follow God's adversary, Satan. We can choose God and good, or Satan/self and evil. Please remember that the choices we make on this earth will determine our eternal destiny – Heaven with the Lord or a place of eternal torment separated from God.

I would like to add that making no choice **is** actually making a choice. A person must actively and intentionally purpose in their mind and heart to love, follow, and obey Christ in order to be saved.

Romans 8:9, 14-15 - 9 But ye are not in the flesh, but in the Spirit, if so be that the Spirit of God dwell in you. Now if any man have not the Spirit of Christ, he is none of his. ... 14 For as many as are led by the

Spirit of God, they are the sons of God. 15 For ye have not received the spirit of bondage again to fear; but ye have received the Spirit of adoption, whereby we cry, Abba, Father.

How wonderful is this? Once we are filled with God's Holy Spirit, we become a child of the living God! This means that **only** those people who are filled with God's Holy Spirit can be a child of God and as such, are our sisters and brothers in Christ.

The next question that begs to be answered is, "How can we know if any person in particular is filled with the Holy Spirit thus being a brother or sister in Christ?" The short answer can be found in the Bible where it says that we will know them by their fruit.

2 Corinthians 5:17 - 17 Therefore if any man [be] in Christ, [he is] a new creature: old things are passed away; behold, all things are become new.

Matthew 12:50 – [Jesus Speaking] 50 For whosoever shall do the will of my Father which is in heaven, the same is my brother, and sister, and mother.

Matthew 7:15-23 [Jesus Speaking] - 15 Beware of false prophets, which come to you in sheep's clothing, but inwardly they are ravening wolves. 16 Ye shall know them by their fruits. Do men gather grapes of thorns, or figs of thistles? 17 Even so every good tree bringeth forth good fruit; but a corrupt tree bringeth forth evil fruit. 18 A good tree cannot bring forth evil fruit, neither [can] a corrupt tree bring forth good fruit. 19 Every tree that bringeth not forth good fruit is hewn down, and cast into the fire. 20 Wherefore by their fruits ye shall know them. 21 Not every one that saith unto me, Lord, Lord, shall enter into the kingdom of heaven; but he that doeth the will of my Father which is in heaven. 22 Many will say to me in that day, Lord, Lord, have we not prophesied in thy name? and in thy name have cast out devils? and in thy name done many wonderful works? 23 And then will I profess unto them, I never knew you: depart from me, ye that work iniquity.

What we can gather from all of this is that Spirit-filled believers are our true brothers and sisters in Christ. Once a person is filled with the Holy Spirit, they become a new creature in Christ. They will seem different from how they were before being born again. They will display the fruits of the Spirit such as love, joy, peace, kindness, patience or long suffering, gentleness and self-control. They will obey the Word of God, and the desire of their heart will be to **do** the will of the Father. As human beings, we might make some mistakes, but it will **never** be the intention of our heart to displease or disobey God. And, a true born-again believer in Christ will be quick to repent of any sin or disobedience.

Before we seek to determine who is and is not our brother or sister in Christ, we need to ask ourselves first, "Am I truly a born-again brother or sister in Christ?" This may be the most important question you can ask yourself in terms of where you will spend eternity.

NOTES FROM CATHERINE:

I believe that George had two main reasons for including this particular teaching.

First, George's heart was always to bring others

to Christ for their eternal salvation. It was his desire that every person with whom he spoke, and who claimed to be a Christian, would be able to examine themselves to see if they were truly saved. Please, do not fear self-reflection. You need to know that you are truly saved. This is what God desires for you!

Second, George wanted to give followers of Christ some biblical parameters in which to assess whether or not another person was truly saved and as such, a trustworthy brother or sister in Christ. Placing one's trust in a false teacher or false Christian can have devastating effects and negative eternal ramifications, particularly for those who are young in their walk with Christ. We are to seek brothers and sisters in Christ for fellowship, and mature brothers and sisters in Christ for counsel and teaching. These will be people who walk the talk! The Bible assures us that we will know them by their fruits, and assessing their fruits as well as our own is what we need to do!

Closing Thoughts & Prayer

by Catherine

Our Lord God loves each and every one of us as His creation. He intentionally planned to suffer and die on the cross for each and every one of us when we were still sinners and undeserving of His love. It is His desire that no one be lost.

After the fall of man in the Garden of Eden, the only way for us to be saved was through Jesus' suffering, spilled blood and death on the cross, resurrection from the dead, and the gift of the infilling of His Holy Spirit.

But here's the catch. We can only be redeemed and saved by actively and intentionally choosing God's plan for our redemption. His plan dictates that we are to believe with our hearts and confess with our mouth that Jesus is the Son of God and was resurrected from the dead. We must repent of sin, change our minds, and stop doing that which is sinful in God's sight. We must love God above all else with our whole heart and out of this love, we must fully obey and serve Him as our sovereign Lord and God. The reward for us making this choice is eternal life spent walking and talking with God on streets of gold!!

That choice is yours to make. Please, choose wisely!

I will end this book with the same prayer of blessing that George prayed at the end of each and every sermon. It is the Aaronic Blessing found in Numbers 6:24-26, from the New King James Version.

> *The LORD bless you and keep you;*
>
> *The LORD make His face shine upon you, And be gracious to you;*
>
> *The LORD lift up His countenance upon you, And give you peace.*

With much love in Christ, until we meet again.

Afterword
George's Last Day: 7/22/22

by Catherine

I wanted to share with all of you reading this book the story of George's last day with us here on earth. Even in the midst of what was a horrifying experience for those of us who were there, we all know that God's hand was upon George even to His last breath. My hope is that the details of this story will draw you closer to the Lord Jesus, comfort you in the storms of your life, and give you the eternal hope that only rests in Jesus.

The story leading up to George's last day on planet earth actually began roughly twenty years prior. When his father was in intensive care in the hospital on life support following a massive stroke, George had prayed a prayer for his father's life. On the night before the family was going to end the life support, George went in to visit his father one last time. He dropped to his knees and prayed that if the Lord would allow his father to live ten more years, then he would give up ten years of his life for this to happen. After this prayer, the room lit up, his father opened his eyes and three days later, walked out of the hospital without any disabilities! According to George, his father lived for almost exactly ten more years after this!

George and I met and married a few years after this incident, and he told me this story. He made it very clear to me that this was an agreement or covenant that he had made with God, and he fully intended to keep his end of it. He was very firm about it, to ensure that I would never pray against it but allow it to remain an agreement between him and God.

Every so often throughout the 17 years that we were married, the Lord would remind George of their agreement and advise him to get his house in order. George would keep me informed whenever this happened. Then, the week before George's last day in this world, he told me that the Lord had shown him that his time was very, very short. George sat me down and discussed what he wanted me to do when the time came. He also added that, if Jesus gave him a choice to stay or return to earth, he was going to stay with the Lord. George's heart was always set on heavenly things!

On that fateful day, George and I were planning on visiting our son, Andrew, and his family, including his wife, Whitney, and their two children, Lucas, who was eight years old, and Ella, who had just turned five years old. The original plan was that we were going to babysit Lucas and Ella for the weekend while their parents went to an out-of-town family wedding. We were planning on arriving around dinnertime.

However, early that morning, our son called to see if we could arrive early. They wanted to invite us out with them for a boat ride and day at the beach on Lake Ontario which was only minutes away from their home. George swiftly decided to put his morning plans on hold, accept the invitation, and enjoy a day at the beach with family. (Note: This was a last-minute change of plans.)

The day was warm but overcast. The boat ride to the beach was pleasant and smooth. As was our routine for boat-ride beach trips, we lugged the beach chairs, toys, and snacks to our favorite area of the beach and the kids ran into the water to play. Ella, the five-year-old, was wearing a life jacket while her big brother, Lucas, the eight-year-old, was not wearing a life jacket. George and I ran into the water after them while Andrew and Whitney set up the chairs on the beach. There was nothing unusual about any of this. We were a happy family enjoying the day together.

This particular area of beach had an expansive sand bar. This caused the water to remain very shallow, less than knee deep, for quite a long distance out into the lake. So, we headed towards where there were some small waves for the kids to play in. On the way, Ella doggie-paddled about six feet away from me. I yelled to her to come back. She spun around and started panicking and screaming, "Mimi, I can't! I can't!" In a moment's time, a sudden rip-tide current ripped the sand bar out from under our feet and we were struggling to remain afloat. I found out later that this is a rare occurrence in Lake Ontario, but that happens every couple of years after intense rainstorms. Indeed, there had been intense rain there the week before.

In that instant, the usually clear lake water became black as night and all at once, angry random waves were pounding us on all sides, along with the water's downward pulling force. I struggled to get to Ella, while George spun around to rescue Lucas. Once I was able to get ahold of Ella, I turned my head to look at the shore and yell for help. Thankfully, George was able to grab ahold of Lucas, and managed to hold him above the water while swimming towards Ella and me. I am not a strong swimmer at all and knowing this, George was working very hard to try to push all of us towards the shore while the rip current was fighting against us and carrying us out further into the darkened lake. When we could catch our breath, we kept on yelling for help, but no one heard or saw what was happening.

Whitney is a wonderful mother and usually never takes her eyes off of the kids for even a moment while they are in the water, even when we grandparents are with them. But on this particular day, at the exact moment the sand bar vanished beneath our feet, some of Andrew and Whitney's friends stopped by to talk to them and blocked their view of us in the water. They could not see us at all, and they could not hear our cries for help.

As we continued to struggle, George managed to push Ella closer to the shore. In her life jacket, she was safe from submersion under the water, but she was getting pounded by the waves, was very frightened, and kept screaming for help. Then all of a sudden, I heard Lucas scream, "*I can't brea.....!*" I turned my head towards the voice, and I saw the top of his head going under the water. In a fraction of a second, my left arm went under the water, grabbed his upper arm, and lifted him up over my head.

I looked up at Lucas in shock and disbelief! Remember, the water was black with pounding waves, and I could not see him at all under the water! There is truly NO WAY that I could have blindly reached for Lucas, grabbed his arm, and lifted him up over my head while I was barely above the water myself! In addition to this, I could not feel Lucas' arm in my hand, and I did not feel the weight of this eight-year-old boy that I was now holding over my head while marginally treading water! There is no doubt in my mind that this was done by the hand of God or a guardian angel! I can only say, "Thank you, Lord, for your provision and protection!"

Next, I looked over my left shoulder to see if I could find George. He was right next to me, under the water making his way to the top. I could see him clearly. It was as if a single ray of sunshine was illuminating his face under the water. His eyes were open, and his face was peaceful while he calmly stroked his arms in the water. This made no sense to me! He was under the water and should have been struggling to get that next breath of air, but he wasn't. All of a sudden, his arms stopped moving and his body drifted downwards while the ray of sunshine vanished. The water went back to being black and angry.

While the kids and I continued to scream for help, a woman was on the sandbar with her two children. She heard our cries and sent her kids to the beach for help while she jumped into that awful current to help me get Ella to safety on the shore. She reached Ella and kept yelling to me, "I've got her, hang on, help is coming!" I was exhausted and her encouragement helped me to keep going! Now, as God would have it, the woman who jumped in the current with me is a Christian Pastor's wife. Just like me! She later told me that this was not the beach they typically visited, but that they had made a last-minute decision to stay there for the day. God is truly sovereign and provided His servants to help us!

A few minutes later, a motorized rowboat came to our aid. They had to proceed very slowly in order to keep control of the boat in the midst of the waves so that they would not hit us. We grabbed onto the boat, and they brought us to where the shallow sand bar still remained so that we could put our feet down. The owner of that boat later told me that he did not want to go boating that day at all. His family practically forced him to go to the beach and had convinced him that morning to go for just one more boat ride. Again, God provided rescuers for us at just the right time!

At the very moment that the boat successfully brought us to the place where we could put our feet on solid ground, the friends who had been visiting with Andrew and Whitney went on their way, and Andrew and Whitney finally saw what was happening. Needless to say, they came running!

Everyone was accounted for, except for George. There was no sight of him anywhere. He was gone. We were catching our breath and getting settled on the shore, but George was still missing and the likelihood of finding him was slim at best. The rip current could have taken him anywhere, including deep under the water. I prayed to the Lord to allow his body to be found. God faithfully answered my prayer and George's body was recovered within a few hours after the incident. Again, thank you Lord for answering our prayers!

In all the shock of the situation and intense grief over losing my beloved husband, I sought the Lord with all my heart. The Lord faithfully answered me by saying, "Stay the course."

As part of a post-traumatic type of response, the events of that day kept uncontrollably playing over and over in my mind for months. I always remembered it exactly the same each time. I could not see Lucas next to me under the blackened water at all, but I could see George clearly behind me under the water. It never struck me as odd until the first time I told the story to my new pastor. Then, it hit me like a ton of bricks!

Remember, the day had been overcast, so there was no sun. The single ray of sunshine illuminating George's face under the blackened water was not the light of the sun. It was the LIGHT! In His infinite mercy, the Lord had not only warned me that George would be coming home to Him soon, but also allowed me to see the exact moment when George's spirit left his body and went towards the Light of God! The look of peace on George's face was indescribable! What an amazing gift God gave me!

God is real. Jesus is real. Jesus is the Light and the Light is real!! In good times and in bad, our Lord and Savior, Jesus, remains in control. We may not always like or understand what is going on, but we know the One who does and that is all we really need!

There is no doubt in my mind that George heard these words from the Lord, "Welcome home, good and faithful servant." He had served the Lord with all his heart during his life and ultimately, gave his life to save the lives of others. He served the Lord to His last breath!

As for me, I know that the Lord has more work for me to do in this world for His kingdom. I learned so much from George during our time together on this earth. I know that I was prepared "for such a time as this" by the Lord as well as my husband. I look forward to the day when I, myself, am called home to be with the Lord. I long to hear Jesus say to me, "Well done, good and faithful servant". And after that, I look forward to being with George once again.

To God be all glory!

Ella, Cathy, Lucas, and George

ABOUT THE AUTHORS

George D. Vitetta's life was radically changed when he discovered that truly walking with God was so different from what he had experienced in today's church. As a Pastor, George's passion was to teach the Bible to inspire everyone towards their own personal relationship with God through faith in Jesus Christ. George passed on to be with the Lord in July of 2022.

Catherine M. Vitetta co-pastored their home church and community outreaches. Her first book, *Ready for the King*, was released in 2023. She is co-author of her husband's book, completing it in loving memory of him after his passing to see God's purpose for the book fulfilled.

Made in the USA
Columbia, SC
24 October 2023

24567653R00087